Public Utility Rate Making in an Energy-Conscious Environment

Other Titles in This Series

Westview Special Studies in
Natural Resources and Energy Management

Public Utility Rate Making in an
Energy-Conscious Environment
edited by Werner Sichel

This collection of papers by some of America's most
respected scholars and practitioners in the field of public
utility regulation provides an up-to-date analysis of urgent
problems and proposed remedies concerning the electricity and
natural gas industries. The authors--two academic economists,
a professor of law, a practicing attorney and consumer advocate,
a state government regulator, an energy economist at the
national level, and two economic researchers in the private
sector--offer differing perspectives concerning major aspects
of the "energy crisis" that faces the U.S. today. Taken
together, their contributions form an excellent synthesis of
modern thinking in the public utility regulation field.

Werner Sichel, professor of economics at Western Michigan
University, received his Ph.D. from Northwestern University.
He has served as a consultant to business firms, consumer groups,
and law firms and is the author or editor of ten books and
numerous articles in the fields of business and economics.

Public Utility Rate Making in an Energy-Conscious Environment
edited by Werner Sichel

Westview Press / Boulder, Colorado

Copyright © 1979 by Westview Press

Published in 1979 in the United States of America by

    Westview Press, Inc.
    5500 Central Avenue
    Boulder, Colorado 80301
    Frederick A. Praeger, Publisher

Library of Congress Cataloguing in Publication Data
Main entry under title:
Public utility rate making in an energy conscious
    environment.
    (Westview special studies in natural resources and
energy management)
    Includes index.
    1. Electric utilities--United States--Rates--Addresses,
essays, lectures. 2. Gas, Natural--United States--Rates--
Addresses, essays, lectures. 3. Energy policy--United
States--Addresses, essays, lectures.
I. Sichel, Werner.
HD9685.U5P83   338.4'3   78-18916
ISBN 0-89158-180-4

Printed and bound in the United States of America

To my father
Joseph Sichel
on his eightieth birthday

Contents

Acknowledgments

The essays in this book were originally prepared for presentation to the Seventh Michigan Conference on Public Utility Economics which took place in the spring of 1977 at Wayne State University in Detroit, Michigan.

The conference was made possible by a grant from Michigan Bell Telephone Company to the University of Michigan and was under the direction of the Inter-University Committee on Public Utility Economics chaired by Dean William Haber from the University of Michigan. Others who served on the committee were Professor Thomas G. Gies, University of Michigan; Mr. Lloyd J. Haynes, vice-president for revenues and public relations, Michigan Bell Telephone Company; Professor Barbara Murray, University of Detroit; Professor William G. Shepherd, University of Michigan; Professor Harry Trebing, Michigan State University; and myself. I am grateful to all of these persons. Their help in topic and speaker selection was of enormous value.

I also thank a number of other people who played an important role in making the conference a success and this volume possible. Professor David J. Smyth, chairman of the Economics Department at Wayne State University, acted as our gracious host. Mrs. Elizabeth T. Bevins, secretary to Dean William Haber, assisted with the countless administrative tasks that needed to be done. Mrs. Cress Strand and Mrs. Christine Truckey did the typing, retyping, and all the sundry chores associated with the preparation of the manuscript.

My greatest debt, of course, is to the authors whose essays appear in this volume. They visited Wayne State University and delivered a version of the essays found in this book. They also subjected themselves to a barrage of questions and engaged in what amounted to a two-day dialogue with some 40 or so public utility regulation economists.

Last, I sincerely thank my wife Beatrice, my daughter Linda, and my son Larry, who, as always, provided the emotional support that I require to carry on my work.

Werner Sichel
Kalamazoo, Michigan

About the Editor and Contributors

Werner Sichel is professor of economics at Western Michigan University. He received the Ph.D. in economics from Northwestern University in 1964. He has served as a consultant to several business firms, consumer groups, and law firms. Dr. Sichel is past president of the Economics Society of Michigan. In 1968-1969 he was a Fulbright-Hays senior lecturer at the University of Belgrade in Yugoslavia. He is a frequent contributor to various business and economics journals, especially in the field of industrial organization. He is the author of *Basic Economic Concepts* (2d. edition, 1977), and the editor of *Industrial Organization and Public Policy: Selected Readings* (1967), *Antitrust Policy and Economic Welfare* (1970), *Public Utility Regulation: Change and Scope* (1975), *The Economic Effects of Multinational Corporations* (1975), *Salvaging Public Utility Regulation* (1976), and *Economic Advice and Executive Policy* (1978).

Paul L. Joskow is professor of economics at Massachusetts Institute of Technology. He holds a doctorate degree from Yale University. He is co-editor of the *Bell Journal of Economics and Management Science* and serves on the editorial board of *Land Economics*. He serves as a consultant to The Rand Corporation, the Organization for Economic Cooperation and Development (OECD), and the Ford Foundation. Dr. Joskow is the author of a large number of articles in economics journals including the *American Economic Review, Journal of Political Economy, Land Economics, Bell Journal,* and the *International Economic Review.*

Roger Koenker is a member of technical staff of the Economics Research Department, Bell Laboratories, Murray Hill, New Jersey. He received the A.B. degree from Grinnell College in 1969 and the Ph.D. in economics from the University of Michigan in 1974. He taught economics and econometrics at the University of Illinois at Champaign-Urbana before joining Bell Laboratories in 1976.

David Sibley is a member of technical staff of the Economics Research Department, Bell Laboratories, Murray Hill, New Jersey. He received the B.A. degree from Stanford University in 1969 and the Ph.D. in economics from Yale University in 1973.

Lawrence Kumins is energy economist, Congressional Research Service, U.S. Library of Congress. Previously he was an economic consultant for a major oil company, a business analyst for several other firms, an economist for the New York Stock Exchange, and assistant to the chief economist of the Federal Power Commission.

Philip J. Mause of Nathan, Mause, and Thorpe, Attorneys at Law, Washington, D.C., held until recently the position of staff attorney, Environmental Defense Fund, where he was heavily involved as an intervener in electric utility rate cases. Before that he was associate professor of law at the University of Iowa. During 1971-1972 he held the Russell Sage Residency in Law and Social Science at the John F. Kennedy School of Government, Harvard University. In 1968 he earned an L.L.B. degree, magna cum laude, *Law Review*, from Harvard University. Mr. Mause's articles have appeared in the Iowa, Minnesota, and Harvard *Law Reviews*.

Alfred L. Parker is professor of economics at the University of New Mexico. He previously taught at Oklahoma State University, Ohio State University, and Otterbein College. He has served as a consultant to the New Mexico Bureau of Business Research, the New Mexico Environmental Institute, the Governor's (New Mexico) Energy Task Force, and the Governor's (New Mexico) Energy Conservation Committee. He frequently presents testimony as expert witness in utility cases. Dr. Parker has authored numerous articles in academic journals on various topics including federal treble damage actions and the energy crisis.

Thomas D. Morgan is professor of law at the University of Illinois. He previously taught at Cornell University Law School and was special assistant to the Assistant Secretary of Defense. He holds a J.D. degree with honors from the University of Chicago Law School. Professor Morgan is the author of several articles in various law reviews and is the developer of a computer game for law students studying regulated industries. His books include *Economic Regulation of Business: Cases and Materials* (1976) and *Professional Responsibility: Problems and Materials* (1976).

Eric J. Schneidewind is director of policy at the Michigan Public Service Commission. He was awarded a law degree from the University of Michigan in 1970 and admitted

to the Michigan Bar in 1971. Before joining the Public
Service Commission, Mr. Schneidewind was with the Legal
Liaison Division of the Michigan Department of Social Services,
the Securities Bureau of the Michigan Department of Commerce,
the Michigan Housing Development Bureau, and was deputy
director for Policy and Consumer Protection at the Michigan
Insurance Bureau.

Introduction

Werner Sichel

Of the several crises in which U.S. society now finds itself, the so-called energy crisis probably receives the most
public attention. The severe winters of 1977 and 1978 have
bestowed a considerable amount of hardship on many American
citizens. In some states, commercial and industrial enter-
prises have been subjected to curtailment and interruption of
certain energy sources; they, along with residential consumers
throughout the nation, have had to pay sharply higher prices
for the energy they use.

Public utility regulators, both federal and state, have
been called upon to alleviate this situation. Many observers
believe that what is needed is a comprehensive energy plan
that would provide relief through federal government determination of the supply and utilization of energy. Others fear
more government regulation and favor greater reliance on the
free market. These "deregulationists" point to the record of
government intervention and argue that such federal measures
as the Connally Hot Oil Act, the percentage depletion allowance,
mandatory oil import quotas, natural gas price controls, and
crude oil price controls have not had a beneficial effect,
but rather have contributed to the energy problem the United
States is now suffering.

Besides the controversy surrounding the optimum degree of
government regulation, several more limited controversies are
also raging. These concern the type of government regulation
that ought to be practiced in markets where it seems desirable
not to rely completely on free competition. One set of controversies, the one with which the contributors to this volume
are most concerned, involves the level and structure of prices.

The level of prices refers to the overall return to public
utility firms. These have been discussed for many years in the
context of such issues as the determination of utility firm
costs, the determination of utility firm rate base, and the
determination of a fair rate of return to the utility firm.
A particular rate level may stem from any one of a variety of
alternative rate structures. Different customers may be

charged different prices and different prices may be charged
to the same customers for different units of output and at
different times. Such structural issues as average cost
pricing versus marginal cost pricing, increasing versus decreasing block rates, and uniform versus time-of-day pricing
have received more attention in recent years.

The seven essays in this book deal with either the
electricity industry or the natural gas industry. Two authors
discuss rate making in electric utilities and two in the
natural gas industry. A fifth contributor evaluates a particular method of regulating price that has been applied to the
electricity industry in one state, and a sixth expert analyzes
the procedural impediments to changing rates in public utility
industries, including electricity and natural gas. The last
essay focuses on the relationship between conservation efforts
and prices of electricity and natural gas.

"Electric Utility Rate Structures in the United States:
Some Recent Developments," by Paul Joskow, is a discussion of
the progress made by state regulatory bodies in determining
the best rate structure to be used by electricity firms.
Joskow points out that until recently, state public utility
commissions were primarily concerned with overall revenue
requirements and not with rate structure at all. He reports
that some substantial reforms have taken place and that a much
more enlightened breed of regulators is considering such
variables as marginal cost, demand elasticity, and time-of-day
pricing, all aimed at increasing economic efficiency. Joskow
links these reforms to a number of recent developments, including the sharp inflation of the early 1970s, which spawned
many electric rate cases as firms were attempting to raise
rates to offset higher unit costs; the environmental movement,
which was rate-structure oriented; and the energy crisis,
which aroused concern over the growth of electricity consumption.

Joskow discusses the difficulties and frustrations involved in implementing reform and presents some data to show
the extent to which regulatory reform has taken place. He
concludes on a note of optimism, predicting that state regulatory progress will continue and even accelerate.

The second essay, "Nonuniform Pricing Structures in
Electricity," is by two Bell Laboratory research economists,
Roger Koenker and David Sibley. Whereas Joskow generally
referred to the more sophisticated pricing structures that are
now understood and dealt with by public utility regulators,
Koenker and Sibley key in specifically on such structures as
the setting of nonuniform electricity prices for different
residential customer groups.

Nonuniform pricing refers to setting rates so that the
customer's cost of consuming a given amount of electricity is
not simply proportional to the amount that he consumes. It
differs from the two-part tariff pricing scheme in that it
does not include an entry fee; rather, it sets high marginal

prices for the first few kilowatt hours of electricity consumption. Both schemes set prices equal to marginal cost for
higher ranges of consumption so that the welfare optimum may
be approached without any government subsidies.

Koenker and Sibley provide a numerical analysis involving
simulation techniques to attain insights into nonlinear pricing
structures. They derive the optimal nonuniform price formula
with which they can compute optimal nonlinear price schedules
using demand and cost data for residential electricity. The
work is based on several essential assumptions, including
(1) the regulatory commission maximizes social welfare
(aggregate consumer surplus plus profit) and (2) the consumer
maximizes net consumer surplus. They also assume that the
particular rate structure that is chosen will effect the
number of subscribers to a particular utility firm. They
recognize that this is a less tenable assumption for residential
than for industrial customers but in the absence of confirming
or denying evidence rely on that important assumption.

The third and fourth essays concern the pricing of natural
gas. Lawrence Kumins evaluates the problems and options that
confront U.S. natural gas regulators at the federal level, and
Philip Mause keys in on the virtues of applying marginal
cost analysis to the setting of prices for natural gas sales
at the state level.

Kumins reviews the current regulatory system in light of
past developments. The 1938 Natural Gas Act, which granted the
Federal Power Commission the power to regulate interstate
sales of natural gas, for 16 years limited regulation to the
rates paid to interstate pipelines selling to distribution
companies. In 1954, however, the Supreme Court presented a
new interpretation that resulted in the regulation of wellhead
prices. First, regulation was on a producer-by-producer basis,
next on the basis of a producing area, and since 1974 on a
nationwide basis. In addition, the concept of pricing based
on gas vintage (old gas versus new gas) was introduced in 1965.
Kumins examines the performance of the industry under these
regulatory conditions and observes that regulation has
apparently kept natural gas prices down during the 1960s.
After the Arab oil embargo of 1973, a very obvious "shortfall"
appeared. Production had decreased, demand had increased,
and the price, of course, went up. Kumins argues that while
the nonregulated intrastate gas prices went up more than the
regulated interstate gas prices, the latter have protected the
intrastate gas markets from nationwide demand and thus much
greater increases in price.

In taking a careful look at production trends in natural
gas, Kumins notes that proven reserves peaked in 1967 and that
the apparent post-embargo upsurge in the drilling of gas wells
may just be an attempt to change "old" gas into "new" gas
rather than reflect a meaningful increase in the supply. He
looks at what production levels of natural gas can realistically

be expected and presents a chronological summary of forecasts of future production which indicates lower levels in the not too distant future. Kumins argues that resource considerations should have a central role in shaping national gas policy. Because his findings lead to the conclusion that large production increases above the present rate seem unlikely, he advocates a policy of discouraging gas consumption and allocating available supplies to the highest priority users. The setting of these priorities may be determined through two very different basic approaches: (1) "administrative end-use measures" and (2) "market determined allocation using the price mechanism." While Kumins is careful to hedge when the evidence is inconclusive, he clearly expresses more confidence in administrative non-price means than in the free market. He discusses the positive relationship between natural gas prices and the cost of input factors as well as the element of holding back production in anticipation of higher market prices. He reviews some demand elasticity studies for natural gas, stressing that demand is fairly inelastic in the short run. On the basis of these discussions he finds that conservation through regulation is superior to price as a conservation tool.

Kumins opposes deregulation on the grounds that the economic impact from further gas price increases would be very disruptive. He estimates that energy price increases during 1974 and 1975 accounted for about one-fourth of the U.S. inflation and one-half of the decline in U.S. gross national product during that period. He fears that deregulation would cause an upward spurt in intrastate prices, necessitate renegotiation of many existing contracts, and add to the incentive to redrill old fields.

Kumins asserts that there really is no truly free competitive market for oil and gas in the world today and that either the U.S. government sets maximum gas prices or U.S. citizens pay minimum gas prices set indirectly by OPEC.

Philip Mause, in his essay on natural gas rate making, stays away from the regulation-deregulation debate; instead he examines the question of rate structure, specifically the rates charged to industrial, commercial, and residential users of natural gas. His primary concern is that consumers are presented with the correct price signals so that efficient use of natural gas is encouraged. Such trade-offs as those between alternative fuels or between purchasing more gas and adding insulation are based on the structure of natural gas rates. Declining block rates and volume discounts provide exactly the opposite incentives than are desirable for our economy.

Mause analyzes the structure of natural gas costs in the United States and points out some of the peculiar characteristics of this industry. The existence of long-term contracts causes the average cost to be quite low, but due to expensive

new sources of supply, marginal cost is very high. Exactly
the opposite is the case in the distribution system; embedded
pipeline costs are very high, while the marginal cost of gas
flowing through the pipelines is very low. Also, other
peculiarities such as the weather sensitivity of demand,
the close relationship to OPEC oil, and the long term wasteful
customs surrounding the consumption of gas are introduced by
Mause. He explains that the most common pattern for pricing
new sources of natural gas is to "roll in" the costs of the
new gas with the costs of the already flowing gas and to charge
consumers an average price qualified by a volume discount or
declining block rates. Mause would instead like to apply
marginal cost pricing. He enumerates a number of problems
that would be encountered, but still contends that an opportunity cost benchmark must be reflected in the rate structure.
Mause offers a number of practical solutions including incremental pricing, inverted rates, and lump sum rebates, which,
while not corresponding perfectly to marginal cost pricing,
would move us a lot closer to it. In an appendix, Mause
provides a comparison of a typical rate structure to a rate
structure based on the marginal cost principle.

"An Evaluation of the New Mexico Public Utility Rate
Indexing Experiment" is by Alfred Parker, a close observer of
the New Mexico public utility regulation scene for a number of
years. Parker describes and carefully evaluates the Cost of
Service Index experiment. Since only two years had passed
between the time that the New Mexico Public Service Commission
adopted the Cost of Service Index and the time that Parker
evaluated it, it may be desirable to reevalaute it after some
additional experience.

Parker explains that the adoption of the index was a reaction to a long rate proceeding and the anticipation of many
more like it. The index was seen as a way to cope with
regulatory lag, to minimize revenue requirements, to encourage
company efficiency, and to promote regulatory efficiency.
It provides for automatic quarterly adjustments in the base
rate for electricity when net income available for common equity
provides a rate of return above or below the allowed rate of
return.

Parker examines the price adjustments made during the
first two years of operation and finds that the index has tended
to stabilize Public Service Company of New Mexico's return on
equity. He reports that this company's stock price went up
relative to other utility firms and that its price-earnings
ratio increased. He then provides an estimate of the amount
of savings in the cost of equity capital that has allegedly
resulted from the use of the index. He similarly makes the
case for the index being responsible for substantial savings
in the cost of debt capital and provides an estimate of that
amount. Finally, Parker discusses the apparent impact of the
index on the efficiency of Public Service Company of New Mexico

and of the commission. He enumerates the provisions in the
index that were designed to provide an incentive to the firm
to keep its costs down and finds that they have been effective.
Even clearer is the contribution that the index has made to
the more efficient operation of the New Mexico Public Service
Commission. Parker finds that the commission resources that
have been freed through the elimination of traditional rate
proceedings have gone into a number of important new programs
which enhance the reliability of future service and improve
customer utilization.

     In "Procedural Impediments to Optimal Ratemaking,"
Thomas Morgan suggests that if all states adopted indexing
for all public utility industries, his essay would be of little
consequence. However, the New Mexico Cost of Service Index
is unique and furthermore applied only to the electricity
industry. Thus the issue that Morgan deals with is lively
and vitally important. His essay addresses the problem of
regulatory lag not only in electricity and natural gas cases,
but in other public utility industries as well.

     Morgan discusses what he believes are the root causes of
procedural impediments in utility rate cases. He contends
that the legal profession has substantial control of regulatory lag, but that one should not assume that the effects of
regulatory lag are altogether detrimental to society. The
presence of a lag between experienced costs and allowed rates,
for example, can create an incentive for utility firms to keep
their costs down. Also, high quality regulation has to take
some time, so a virtually delay-free system may simply indicate
that virtually no regulation takes place.

     Morgan presents a good summary of the nature and extent
of current rate-making delays at the FPC, FCC, ICC, and CAB
and on the state level. He finds that the greatest delay does
not take place at the stage of the formal hearing, but rather
before the hearing when the commission staff and interveners
review the data and after the hearing when a decision is being
reached. He enumerates a number of "solutions" that have been
offered, including the setting of a time limit for the decision
process, the discouragement of intervener involvement, the
elimination of some steps in the decision process, decreased
formality, more careful tracking of cases, and automatic
adjustment. Morgan contends, however, that these are not
adequate solutions since the problem is greater than merely
"a few procedural impediments." He would instead like to see
a whole new strategy of rate making that entails (1) more
extensive use of rule making to avoid case-by-case adjudication
and thus more carefully address the fundamental issues,
(2) periodic submission of utility company data to the regulating commission so that it can study the pertinent facts on
a continuous basis, and (3) encouragement of settlement of rate
cases. Morgan is convinced that the adoption of these three
fundamental changes would substantially decrease regulatory

lag, yet not abandon high-quality regulation.

The last chapter, "New Economics in Energy," is by Eric Schneidewind, who contends that a new approach should be taken by regulators who have in recent years been frustrated in performing the task assigned to them. Astronomical increases in the energy costs of utility firms have put severe and almost continuous pressure on regulators to allow rate increases. Since the cost pressures are greatest at the margin--exotic new gas supplies and electricity from new generating plants--Schneidewind suggests that the most cost-effective "production" of energy is from conservation. He examines a number of specific programs and plans in different geographic areas of the United States and concludes that the price increases justify significant new expenditures on energy conservation. The price and cost estimates that he presents for the state of Michigan lead him to state that utility firms could obtain gas at a lower cost by literally giving away residential conservation devices than by drilling a well or importing the gas. Schneidewind predicts that utility firms and those who regulate them will have to adopt more unconventional means such as conservation in an effort to "produce" the energy that is required to maintain the standard of living to which Americans have become accustomed.

Taken together, the seven essays in this volume compose a very good synthesis of current, progressive thinking in the public utility regulation field. The authors, as indicated above, are a heterogeneous group, and they offer different perspectives concerning some major aspects of the energy crisis that faces the United States today.

1
Electric Utility Rate Structures in the United States: Some Recent Developments

Paul L. Joskow

INTRODUCTION

The underlying theoretical rationale for peak load pricing of electricity based on marginal cost principles has been part of the economics literature since the early 1950s. The basic theoretical work in the area took place simultaneously and to a large extent independently in the United States, England, and France during the 1950s and 1960s. Useful extensions of the basic theoretical constructs have continued until the present day.[1] Yet, while the theory of marginal cost pricing was applied to the development of actual electricity price structures in England and France beginning in the 1950s, the impact on electricity pricing in the United States has only become important in the past few years. As recently as five years ago, concepts such as marginal cost, demand elasticity, and economic efficiency rarely if ever found their way into regulatory proceedings dealing with electricity pricing. To-day, these concepts are not only being used routinely in many states, but actual time-of-day rates based on marginal cost pricing principles have been approved in a number of juris-dictions. In addition, millions of dollars are being spent annually by the federal government to finance time-of-day rate experiments, to gather information necessary to estimate time-of-day demand elasticities, and to encourage state regulatory commissions to utilize these concepts in setting electricity rates. This is not to say either that the under-lying concepts of marginal cost pricing theory have been accepted by a majority of state commissions or that actual implementation as yet affects more than a small proportion of consumers. Neither is the case. However, compared to the situation that existed as recently as five years ago, sub-stantial progress has been made on the conceptual level, and implementation is proceeding at a slow but steady pace. There is no question but that the gradual absorption of these principles and concepts by state regulatory commissions repre-sents the most important state regulatory innovation to occur

1

in the United States in many years.

In this chapter, I will discuss the events that set the stage for this important reform in state regulation of electric rates, how far commissions have come in implementing rate structure reform proposals, what problems have stood in the way of more rapid implementation, and the directions in which rate reform appears to be headed.

THE SEEDS OF REFORM

Prior to 1972, concepts of economic efficiency, marginal cost, demand elasticity, and peak load pricing were foreign to most state regulatory commissions. As I have indicated elsewhere, state regulation of electricity rates was probably best characterized during the 1960s as regulation by benign neglect rather than vigorous and continuous profit and rate structure regulation.[2] To the extent that rates were regulated, commissions tended to focus primarily on issues of overall revenue requirements and rate level rather than on rate structure issues. The current movement toward marginal cost pricing and peak load pricing does not represent a movement from one rate structure methodology to another, but rather a movement from *no* specific commission-inspired rate structure methodology to *some* cost-based rate structure methodology. It was not uncommon prior to 1972 to find that neither the commissions nor the electric utilities they regulated had any consistent set of principles to guide the construction of rate structures after a decision on the appropriate revenue requirements for the utilities was determined. The setting of the rate structure was left primarily to the regulated firms themselves, and any underlying methodology that was used was rarely if ever presented in public.

There are a number of economic and political events that began in the early 1970s. These events led public utility commissions to abandon their previous neglect of rate structure issues and forced them both to consider rate structure determination more carefully in regulatory hearings and to develop basic principles on which such rate structure determinations were to be made.

Inflation and the Rapid Increase in Formal Regulation

Beginning in the late 1960s and accelerating in the 1970s, the increased costs of productive inputs began to outrun both economies of scale and improvements in generating efficiency. Through most of the 1960s, the electric utility industry experienced declining unit costs, increasing prices, and little formal regulatory review of prices and profits (see Tables 1 and 2). However, as average costs began to increase in the late 1960s, utilities found that their profits began to decline with fixed regulated prices, and they soon found themselves

2

TABLE 1. COST, REVENUE, AND GENERAL RATE REVIEWS OF
U.S. ELECTRIC UTILITY FIRMS, 1963-1975

Year	General rate reviews	Average cost (cents/kwh)	Average revenue (cents/kwh)
1963	3	1.33	1.77
1964	4	1.30	1.73
1965	2	1.27	1.70
1966	5	1.24	1.67
1967	3	1.24	1.66
1968	8	1.24	1.64
1969	19	1.22	1.63
1970	45	1.25	1.68
1971	51	1.34	1.78
1972	94	1.40	1.86
1973	64	1.49	1.97
1974	78	1.96	2.50
1975	114	2.30	2.94

triggering more and more formal regulatory reviews by request-
ing rate increases. State regulatory commissions, which had
been engaged in few formal rate reviews over the previous
fifteen years, rapidly acquired a heavy administrative burden
of rate determination, normally leading to rate increases that
reflected rising production costs and an increase in the cost
of capital.[3]
     The increased regulatory activity had two important
effects. First, it demonstrated quite clearly that the regulatory agencies rarely had any well-defined methodology for
determining the appropriate rate structure. Second, the formal
hearings presented a natural forum for those with particular
objections to the prevailing rate structures to present their
cases. Regulatory commissions, responsible for approving large
and frequent rate increases (no matter how justified), came
under increasing criticism from consumers and government
officials who were not happy about the fact that electricity
rates were rising rapidly, especially after 1973 as oil prices
skyrocketed and interest rates rose. Long ignored and poorly
staffed state regulatory commissions were suddenly drawn into
the spotlight as the primary villains allowing rate increases
to occur (the utilities shared the spotlight). In many cases,

TABLE 2. YIELDS ON DEBT AND RETURNS ON COMMON EQUITY,
U.S. ELECTRIC UTILITY FIRMS, 1963-1975

Year	Yield on electric utility debt	Rate of return on common equity
1963	4.40	11.4
1964	4.55	11.8
1965	4.61	12.2
1966	5.53	12.4
1967	6.07	12.4
1968	6.80	11.9
1969	7.98	11.8
1970	8.79	11.2
1971	7.72	11.0
1972	7.50	11.1
1973	7.91	10.8
1974	9.59	10.2
1975	9.97	10.6

the criticisms of state regulation were justified. A process
that had been inactive for so many years had neither the human
and financial resources nor adequate administrative procedures
to cope effectively with a substantial amount of formal regulation. Calls for regulatory reform began in 1972 and 1973 and
increased dramatically by 1974. The period of the early 1970s
was characterized by an increasing administrative breakdown of
state regulation of electric rates.

The Environmental Movement

Simultaneously with this breakdown in the regulatory
process and the public's confidence (or ignorance[4]) in it, the
environmental movement came into its own. Groups such as the
Environmental Defense Fund and the Sierra Club had identified
the electric utility industry as an important source of
environmental damage. Among their many activities, these
groups became involved in state rate regulation as interveners.[5]
However, their activities were not directed primarily toward
the allowed rate of return, as had often been the case for
interveners in the past; rather, they were concerned with the
rate structure issue. Their position was simple--existing rate

4

structures tended to promote uneconomic levels of electricity consumption. Existing declining block rate structures, which charged lower marginal and average prices as consumption increased, were identified as the causes of uneconomic excessive consumption of electricity. The environmentalists argued that the current structure of prices led to inefficiently low load factors as well as excess demand for electricity, which in turn required unnecessary building of new generating and transmission facilities. Armed with a voluminous amount of economic theory on marginal cost pricing of electricity, knowledge of the peak load pricing systems in England and France,[6] and the obvious fact that most state commissions had not given rate structure issues proper attention, environmental groups presented strong cases for rate structure reform, based on economic principles, before state regulatory commissions.

The receptive hearing that the proponents of rate structure reform have received has not been because commissions suddenly embraced the principles of microeconomic theory. On the contrary, many commissions and certain intervener groups have adopted rate structure reform in general and peak load pricing in particular for what probably have often been the wrong reasons. Often, the commissions were desperately searching for some reform that could get them out of the quagmire that had been caused primarily by inflation. The reasoning went something like this: One of the forces driving rate increases was the growing consumption of electricity that was necessitating the construction of new production equipment, the cost of which was far above the average historical cost of the plant in place. This plant had to be financed in part by new issues of debt and preferred stock at costs greater than the imbedded cost of capital. It was thought that both forces were responsible for forcing commissions to grant large rate increases, to the great displeasure of consumers. Environmentalists proposed rate structure reform that would slow down the rate of growth of peak demand and the need for more expensive plants and equipment, which presumably would also slow down the rate of price increases that commissions would be required to grant companies. Not only might price increases be mitigated, but so would the adverse environmental consequences associated with power plant construction. Commissions therefore saw a chance of reducing two sources of complaints at the same time.

The early concentration by environmental groups on residential rates and associated proposals for inverted rates reinforced the interest of state commissions, because this approach also seemed to be a way of eliminating the burden on low-income consumers who were presumed also to be small users of electricity.[7] This early, and I believe ill-advised, concentration on residential rates and associated proposals for inverted rates have since been largely abandoned by environmental groups. For an administrative system seeking some kind of reform to alleviate its problems, these early proposals were attractive. In reality, however, the fundamental problems associated with administrative price regulation in a world of rapid inflation could never reasonably have been expected to be eliminated by this type of rate structure reform, in either the short run or the long run.

Finally, the prospect of eventually adopting a peak load pricing system to provide for rates that varied by time of day and season of the year was seen by some commissions as a way of giving consumers an opportunity to reduce their bills. In the face of rapidly rising electric rates, consumers could shift their consumption patterns from peak periods to offpeak periods.[8]

The Energy Crisis

The final event that helped move the system toward rate structure as well as more general reform was the Arab oil embargo and the rapid rise in oil prices that followed it. Associated energy crises led to a reexamination of a wide range of structural and behavioral issues in all energy industries. The electric utility industry was a natural target for close examination since it consumed more than 25 percent of primary energy inputs in the United States, used prodigious amounts of capital, and had a history of consumption growing at a rate about twice that of energy in general. The Federal Energy Administration (FEA) became interested in reducing the growth rate in electricity consumption, increasing electric utility load factors, and insuring that adequate supplies of electricity would be available in what appeared to be a time when utilities were facing serious difficulties in obtaining the capital required to expand generating capacity.[9]

The FEA's reasons for embracing peak load pricing were varied. Some members of the FEA saw it as a method for load management that would reduce the growth rate in electricity consumption; others saw it as a way to reduce utility capital requirements; and still others saw it as a way to reduce rates for certain classes of consumers. For whatever reasons, the FEA became an important force putting pressure on state regulatory commissions to reform electric power rate structures.

To summarize, the initial movement toward peak load pricing based on marginal cost pricing concepts did not come directly from the electric utilities or from state regulatory commissions. Problems faced by the utility companies, the regulatory commission, and the nation as a whole provided the opportunity for reform of rate structures and other regulatory practices. Environmental groups, academic economists, and economic consultants were able to use this opening to present arguments for rate structure reform based on marginal cost pricing principles, with the ultimate aim of introducing seasonal time-of-day pricing in the United States. Their objectives for reform and the objectives of the regulatory commissions, while not inconsistent, were also far from

6

identical. If the environmentalists and economists pushing
marginal cost principles and peak load pricing had tried to do
this in 1966 rather than in 1973, it almost certainly would
have fallen on deaf ears and been largely unsuccessful.[10]

THE ARGUMENT IS DRAWN

Regulatory commissions searching for regulatory reforms
and a consortium of economists and environmentalists with a
reform proposal dealing with at least some of the concerns of
the regulators have not guaranteed any rapid movement toward
the implementation of the reform proposals. In fact, the
arguments between pro- and anti-marginalists and between those
for and against peak load pricing have been heated and drawn
out. The call for reform has led to either footdragging or
outright opposition from a number of interest groups for a
variety of reasons.

For both those responsible for establishing rates within
the regulated utilities ("ratemen") and those responsible for
regulating rates on the staffs of regulatory commissions, the
proposals called for a dramatic change in the methodology used
in establishing rate structures. The new methodology, although
based on a set of economic principles long known to economists,
was completely foreign to those who had been responsible for
setting rates.[11] The movement toward marginal cost pricing
required both different kinds of expertise than traditional
"ratemen" possessed and implied a certain demystification of the
rate-setting process, which had been passed off as an art
rather than a science. The visceral reaction of most of these
people was negative and was manifested in a number of basic
objections:

1. The economic theory on which marginal cost pricing
   was based was a "textbook exercise" with little
   application in the real world. Concepts of "economic
   efficiency" as an objective were especially attacked.
2. Marginal costs were speculative and depended on
   judgment, whereas historical costs were "real,"
   could be worked with readily, and had served as an
   adequate basis for establishing electricity prices
   for many years.
3. There were numerous ways of calculating marginal costs;
   this would lead to much confusion and great difficulty
   in implementation.
4. Prices based on marginal costs would likely lead to
   a "revenue yield" different from the "allowed
   revenues" determined by the regulatory commission
   prior to the rate structure phase of the case. This
   would require deviations from marginal cost, thus
   mitigating the efficiency arguments.
5. Peak load pricing required information on demand
   elasticity if the effect was to be other than shifting
   the peak from one time period to another.

7

The ongoing argument between the economists and those seeking to debunk the teachings of economic theory is perhaps best illustrated in the landmark *Madison Gas and Electric* case.[12] This was the first major electric rate decision in which a commission recognized the importance of using marginal cost as the basis for establishing rate structures, recognized the possible importance of peak load pricing based on marginal cost, and ordered companies under the commission's jurisdiction to undertake research efforts that would allow the commission to evaluate effectively the feasibility of time-of-day rates. The majority of the commission found that

> the principle of marginal cost pricing is an appropriate guide for the purpose of the design of rates of Madison Gas and Electric Company and other Wisconsin Energy Utilities. Such a principle has been shown to be the most effective way to obtain an efficient allocation of resources and to prevent wasteful use of electric energy.[13]

Further, the commission found that

> implementation of pricing on the basis of LRIC [long-run incremental cost] requires that rates charged peak customers exceed those charged off-peak customers. Full peak-load pricing, including different day and nighttime rates must, for large customers, be implemented without delay. As to smaller customers, the cost of metering is a deterent factor, but experimentation and development of appropriate systems must go forward promptly....[14]

The rates established in this proceeding, based on a long-run marginal cost study produced for Madison Gas and Electric by National Economic Research Associates, Inc., provided a summer/winter rate differential reflecting differences in long-run marginal cost. Existing rates were flattened considerably. The commission indicated that this was the first step toward a more comprehensive use of marginal cost principles and the introduction of time-of-day rates.[15]

In his dissenting opinion, Commissioner Padrutt mirrored the views of those opposing change along these lines in utility companies and regulatory commissions. Regarding the basic underlying principles of economics, his dissent began as follows:

> The testimony and debate presented in this case by the learned economists who participated is strongly reminiscent of the disputes of an earlier age when theologians differed concerning the number of angels who could

occupy the head of a pin. For some 3,000 pages of
testimony and reams of exhibits and studies, the
economic experts who appeared as witnesses leaped
and gamboled, like mountain goats, from peak to crag
to precipice in the rarified upper atmosphere of
theoretical economics. In the meanwhile, those of
us not so well endowed, bearing the burden of formu-
lating a viable and practical rate design, were left
to slog painfully through the foothills below.[16]

With regard to measurement of costs for rate making, he found
the following:

Rates should reflect all tangible, actual, measurable
costs of providing the service. To the extent that
marginal costs include something other than an actual
tangible, measurable cost of production, I am in dis-
agreement with the conclusions of this order....[17]

Regarding the difference between marginal cost and the revenue
requirement, Commissioner Padrutt said,

If given full recognition, LRIC will invariably produce
revenues considerably in excess of revenue requirements.
Probabilities seem to be that LRIC would prove to be
equivalent to revenue requirements about once in a
million times.[18]

With regard to the effects of peak load pricing on system
peak, he found that

its [peak load pricing] theory is simple. Increase the
price of energy at peak load periods to a point which
encourages the customer to defer his use to another,
less costly time. In other words, encourage the house-
wife (for an oversimplified example) to turn the
dishwasher on at 10 p.m., where the "dishwasher peak"
presently exists at 7 p.m. In theory, this is
excellent, but it should be very obvious, that if in
practice the gambit is successful, the ultimate
result wipes out the 7 p.m. peak and builds a new
peak at 10 p.m. This serves to demonstrate the basic
fallacy involved in peak load pricing.[19]

Finally, with respect to demand elasticity, he found

that the elasticity of demand for electricity more
nearly approximates that of the piano wire than
that of the rubber band.[20]

I think it is clear to almost anyone who has studied both

9

the theory and application of marginal cost pricing that at
worst these arguments are specious and at best are true for
any pricing methodology that one chooses. However, since
marginal cost pricing theory and associated peak load pricing
proposals were based on a clear set of economic principles and
involved detailed cost calculations, they were an easy target
for those opposed to change for other reasons and who could
hide behind a *status quo ante* based on no clear and consistent
set of principles or methods for calculation.[21] If marginal
cost pricing principles were going to be introduced, a substantial effort at educating "the old hands" was almost certainly going to be a high priority.

On at least one count the critics of time-of-day pricing
were partially correct. Unfortunately, the early presentations
of rate structure reform emphasized residential rates rather
than industrial rates. Yet it was quite clear that the costs
of the meters required to implement time-of-day pricing system
for residential consumers made it far from obvious that the
benefits that might accrue from a peak load pricing system were
worth the additional metering costs that would be entailed.[22]
This concern was reinforced by reports of the British residential rate experiments, which were widely circulated in the
United States. Those opposed to rate structure reform
naturally chose to emphasize this as a fundamental problem with
the underlying theory rather than a relatively straightforward
question of implementation strategy.

A second problem associated with the early discussion of
the benefits of peak load pricing which continues to this day
has been a tendency to define the benefits of peak load pricing
incorrectly and in such a way as to underestimate them. No
doubt responding to the concerns of regulatory commissions,
environmental groups, and the electric utilities themselves,
proponents have tended to define the benefits in terms of the
reductions in peak demand and associated reductions in capacity
expansion and capital requirements that otherwise would be
entailed.[23] Reductions in the capacity to meet peak demands
represent only part of the benefits of peak load pricing. To
this must be added savings associated with energy consumption
taken at peak periods under current rates whose marginal cost
is greater than the average cost-based price being charged as
well as the benefits that accrue from additional energy consumption that would be encouraged by lowering off-peak rates
to their true marginal social costs. Unfortunately, a great
deal of argument has surrounded what is simply the incorrect
measure of the welfare gain to be attributed to introducing a
system of peak load pricing.

Beyond some of the more narrow concerns and criticisms of
some opponents, both companies and commissions were somewhat
reluctant to move too quickly to an entirely different structure
of rates for another reason. Since there is in fact a non-zero
demand elasticity for electricity, there has been considerable

concern that introducing a time-of-day price structure without
knowing with some degree of accuracy what customer responses
would be makes it difficult to estimate with accuracy what the
actual revenue yield of the new rates would be. Both the
companies and the commissions were concerned that if the
customer response was indeed dramatic, revenues would fall
short of requirements, making the financial situation of the
utilities even worse than it already was at the time such rates
were initially proposed. Such concerns are certainly not
completely unjustified, but they can be dealt with fairly
easily without detailed knowledge of time-of-day price elasticities. In any case, these concerns and those above tended
to favor the "go slow" position, which varied from gradual
reform to no reform, pending the results of detailed and con-
vincing experimental evidence on time-of-day price elasticities.[24]

Perhaps the most vocal criticism came from certain consumer
groups who believed that they would be hurt by time-of-day
pricing based on marginal cost. This fear was based on two
observations, one obvious and the second somewhat more subtle.
Since the existing system overcharged customers who consumed
relatively more electricity at off-peak hours and undercharged
customers who consumed relatively more at on-peak times, we
would expect the latter group to oppose any efforts to move to
a peak load pricing system, since no rational consumer will
want to pay more, whatever the aggregate social benefits might
be. Some opposition to peak load pricing was therefore expected, although in the long run the improved load factors
and lower average costs that would result might benefit a
rather large subset of consumers. However, there has been a
more general opposition from large industrial consumers, including those that might in theory benefit from a peak load
pricing system. This reflects the feeling that since prices
based on marginal costs are likely under current circumstances
to yield revenues greater than those allowed by the commission
to achieve a "fair rate of return" on historical cost,[25]
deviations below marginal cost will be required for all or some
consumption categories. Industrial consumers fear that any
such rebates will almost inevitably be granted to residential
consumers. This would result in the industrial consumers
bearing a greater share of the revenue requirements than they
otherwise would under the current system or than they would
if the peculiarities of original cost rate making did not yield
a "rent" with prices set equal to marginal cost that somehow
had to be distributed to consumers. Traditionally they have
received a share of this "rent" and want to continue to do so.

Unfortunately, rather than presenting their actual
objection, which was simply that they did not want to pay more,
a well-financed group of industrial interveners have attempted
to keep marginal cost pricing principles from being introduced
by attacking the theoretical underpinnings of marginal cost
pricing and the evidence from foreign countries.[26] Originally,

this opposition was directed toward marginal cost pricing in general and toward peak load pricing in particular. Recently it has evolved into an opposition to peak load pricing based on marginal cost in favor of peak load pricing based on average cost. This has occurred even though the theoretical justification for peak load pricing flows naturally from marginalist principles rather than from any theory of average cost pricing ever coherently advanced. When pressed, the basic argument for average cost pricing has been that it is "more pragmatic" because it is based on "actual costs" consistent with those used to determine revenue requirements.

WHERE ARE WE NOW?

Despite all the theoretical literature on peak load pricing that has been developed by economists, as well as the 20 years of experience with peak load pricing in Europe, the first vigorous efforts to encourage regulatory commissions to use these principles as a standard for setting electric rate structures in the United States did not really begin until approximately 1972. Regulatory agencies in the United States are not known for their willingness or ability to make radical departures from existing practice, and peak load pricing has been no exception. Nevertheless, some progress has been made in the past five years.

Table 3 indicates the progress that has been made in the various states. Twelve states have held generic hearings on rate structure issues; in almost all cases, these hearings have given detailed attention to marginal cost pricing principles, the application of these principles in terms of computational procedures, and the feasibility of implementation, including considerations of metering costs and the effects that new rate structures would have on different consumer groups. Perhaps more importantly, in 16 states actual time-of-day rates have been filed by electric utility companies. In addition, the FEA has funded rate experiments in 10 states to evaluate the effects of alternative rate structure methodologies on consumer behavior.

To date, the actual implementation of time-of-day rates has been restricted primarily to industrial customers, although in Vermont an optional time-of-day rate is available to residential customers.[27] For example, Wisconsin Power and Light has implemented time-of-day rates for 130 of its largest industrial and commercial customers. Peak hours were defined as 8 a.m. to 10 p.m., Monday through Saturday except holidays. Energy charges were set at 2.026¢/kwh during the peak period and 1.013¢/kwh during the off-peak period, compared to a uniform energy charge of 1.622¢/kwh under the old rates.[28] As a result, one large consumer in the Wisconsin system has shifted 240 workers from the day shift to the night shift and saved $500,000 in the process.[29]

12

In California, Pacific Gas and Electric has put a time-of-day rate structure into effect that will apply to about 120 of its largest customers. In approving the final rates, the California Public Utilities Commission clearly took marginal cost considerations into account.[30] The time-of-day rates approved in California for large customers are shown in Table 4. The rates involve three time-of-day rate periods, which vary, along with charges, from the summer to the winter season. This rate structure is at least as complicated as the industrial rates available in France under the "Green Tariff" since the 1950s.

In New Mexico, Public Service Company of New Mexico's time-of-day rates apply to only three wholesale customers, representing about 9 percent of the company's peak demand. Yet the company credits these rates with increasing its annual system load factor from 66 percent in 1975 to 70 percent in 1976.[31]

In New York, the Public Service Commission has approved time-of-day rates for about 175 of Long Island Lighting Company's largest industrial and commercial consumers. "The rate is based on marginal costs, and the energy charge...is close to the actual charge as dictated by marginal cost principles. The 40-page order approving the rate was written, Public Service Commission sources say, largely as a brief for time of day rates based on marginal costs that is applicable to other cases."[32]

The movement toward peak load pricing and the use of marginal cost pricing principles is of course not uniform across states. Many states are taking a go-slow or wait-and-see attitude. For example, after conducting a generic hearing on rate design, the Maryland Public Service Commission rejected marginal cost pricing and generally urged a go-slow approach to peak load pricing and other rate structure changes.[33]

Besides the expected problems associated with developing a time-of-day rate-making methodology and opposition of various groups who might be hurt by changes in rate structures, there are a number of other reasons (some alluded to above) for the observed rate of reform. Many regulatory commissions simply do not have the staff expertise to evaluate properly the issues associated with rate structure reform or to supervise properly the calculation of the relevant marginal costs and the establishment of associated rate structures. It is therefore not too surprising that most progress has been made in states like New York, Wisconsin, and California, where commissions have larger, more qualified staffs and the commissioners themselves are better trained to evaluate the issues carefully. (Both the New York and California commissions have members who are economists.[34]) Perhaps one of the hidden benefits associated with the "crises of state regulation" experienced in the past five years and the pressures for rate structure reform has been a general upgrading in both the quality of the commissioners and

TABLE 3. STATE REGULATORY PROGRESS--1976

State	Generic rate hearings	FEA-funded experiments	Utilities ordered to introduce time-of-day pricing before filing again	Time-of-day rates have been submitted
Alabama				
Alaska				
Arizona		X		
Arkansas		X		
California	X	X	X	X
Colorado	X			
Connecticut	X	X	X	X
Delaware			X	X
District of Columbia				
Florida	X		X	X
Georgia			X	X
Hawaii	X			
Idaho				
Illinois	X			X
Indiana				
Iowa				X
Kansas				
Kentucky				
Louisiana				
Maine			X	
Maryland	X			
Massachusetts	X			
Michigan		X	X	X
Minnesota				X

14

TABLE 3 (continued)

State	1	2	3	4
Mississippi				
Missouri				
Montana				
Nebraska				
Nevada				
New Hampshire	X	X		X
New Jersey			X	
New Mexico				
New York	X	X	X	X
North Carolina	X	X	X	X
North Dakota				
Ohio		X		
Oklahoma				
Oregon	X		X	
Pennsylvania	X	X		X
Rhode Island				
South Carolina				
South Dakota				
Tennessee				
Texas				
Utah				
Vermont	X	X	X	X
Virginia			X	X
Washington				
West Virginia				
Wisconsin	X	X	X	X
Wyoming				

Source: National Economic Research Associates.

15

TABLE 4. PACIFIC GAS AND ELECTRIC'S TIME-OF-DAY RATES FOR CUSTOMERS WITH DEMAND OF 4,000 kw/MONTH OR MORE

Interval	Period A	Period B
$/maximum kw demand in each time interval		
On-peak	$3.45	$2.30
Plus partial peak	0.28	0.28
Plus off-peak	..	..
$/kwh in each time interval		
On-peak	$0.01218	$0.01218
Plus partial peak	0.01018	0.01018
Plus off-peak	0.00818	0.00818

Period A: Meter readings May 1-Sept. 30

On-peak--12:20 p.m. to 6:30 p.m. Mon.-Fri. except holidays

Partial peak--8:30 a.m. to 12:30 p.m. Mon.-Fri. except holidays

6:30 p.m. to 10:30 p.m. Mon.-Fri. except holidays

8:30 a.m. to 10:30 p.m. Saturdays except holidays

Off-peak--10:30 p.m. to 8:30 a.m. Mon.-Sat. except holidays

All day Sunday and holidays

Period B: Meter readings Oct. 1-April 30

On-peak--4:30 p.m. to 8:30 p.m. Mon.-Fri. except holidays

Partial peak--8:30 a.m. to 4:30 p.m. Mon.-Fri. except holidays

8:30 p.m. to 10:30 p.m. Mon.-Fri. except holidays

8:30 a.m. to 10:30 p.m. Saturdays except holidays

Off-peak--10:30 p.m. to 8:30 a.m. Mon.-Sat. except holidays

All day Sunday and holidays

Customer charge per meter per month, $715.00.

An "energy cost adjustment" of $0.00816/kwh will be added and a "fuel collection balance adjustment" of $0.0042/kwh will be deducted from each bill.

their staffs and the resources at their disposal for extending their responsibilities and expertise into the rate structure area. The FEA's decision to involve state commissions directly in the rate experiments has helped to reinforce this trend.

Metering capabilities have and will continue to represent an important constraint on the speed with which time-of-day rates can and should be implemented. Most implementation to date has applied to larger customers who already have, or can install at relatively low cost, the required metering equipment to make time-of-day rates possible. Even if justified on cost-benefit grounds, it will take many years for appropriate meters to be installed for the 80 million residential and small commercial customers in the United States. It is almost certain that for many of these customers, the potential gains from time-of-day pricing are simply not worth the additional metering costs entailed. Both on practical grounds and on static efficiency grounds, commissions that have moved toward time-of-day rates have logically moved first on industrial consumers where metering problems are not important.

WHERE ARE WE GOING FROM HERE?

Rate structure reform is here to stay. At both the state and federal level, things have gone too far to turn back. With the completion of the Edison Electric Institute-Electric Power Research Institute study, we will get a better feeling for the posture that the electric utility industry will take. I suspect that it will generally be supportive of additional movements toward time-of-day pricing, but will take a more cautious, go-slow policy than some of us might like. I suspect also that the specific costing methodology to be used for determining rates will remain a matter of some controversy.

I expect to see more commissions ordering utilities to propose time-of-day rates for their largest industrial and commercial consumers. I also expect some commissions to order optional time-of-day rates for residential and commercial customers as has been done in England and France over the years. As more information is gained from rate experiments and as advances in metering technology are realized,[35] I expect that this trend will accelerate. I also have the strong feeling that in the end, it will be marginal cost principles that dictate the structure of electricity rates, primarily because it is marginalist principles that make peak load pricing logical in the first place. Even those who say they are using some average cost pricing principle are in essence looking over their shoulders at marginal cost.

In conclusion, I believe that economists deserve a great deal of credit for the direction that rate reform has taken. Supervening events presented an opportunity to rationalize the rate-making process, and economists had at their disposal a set of consistent principles that could help improve the efficiency with which we produce and consume electricity in the United States. Economists have been able to advance both the theory and application of marginal cost pricing, have helped to structure and evaluate rate experiments, and have brought considerations of demand elasticity, marginal cost, economic efficiency, and cost-benefit considerations to a regulatory system that had too long been dominated by accountants and lawyers. Despite the abuse that economists and economic theory have taken in the process, they have stood up well in the process--progress has been made and more will be made in the future.

NOTES

1. See Joskow (1976) for a brief review of existing literature. See also the important paper by Panzar (1976).

2. See Joskow (1974).

3. The discussion that follows is based on Joskow (1974).

4. It would not be surprising to have found that the vast majority of consumers knew little or nothing about the authorities that were responsible for regulating the prices charged them for electricity.

5. The Environmental Defense Fund was an active participant in the *Madison Gas and Electric* case (Wisconsin Public Service Commission, Order dated August 8, 1974), participated in the generic hearings held by the New York State Public Service Commission, and has been active before the California Public Utilities Commission (see *Electrical Week,* November 29, 1976, p. 3).

6. See Nelson (1964) and National Economic Research Associates (1977).

7. There has been a simultaneous movement for various types of "lifeline" rates in a number of states that have been supported by a variety of consumer groups to give discounts to small users of electricity. The actual residistributive effects of such a scheme are difficult to assess (see Pace, 1975). The objectives of those advocating rate reform for residistributive purposes and those advocating reform on efficiency grounds are clearly different, although many commissions have tended to get them confused or to link them together so as to deal with both interest groups.

8. This was giving a carrot to groups seeking rate reform based on efficiency considerations and those seeking rate reform based on income distribution considerations.

9. See Joskow and MacAvoy (1975).

10. The contrast between electricity rates in the United States and those in Europe and the failure to use marginalist principles in the United States had already been well documented (see Clemens, 1963, and Shepherd, 1966).

11. Although the very kinds of analysis needed for calculating the relevant marginal costs had been conducted for many years within many companies, they had been done by the system planning department rather than the rate department. If the close link between pricing and planning that has existed in France had also existed in the United States, some of the purely bureaucratic problems might have been minimized and an easier transition been accomplished.

12. Public Service Commission of Wisconsin, August 8, 1974. Application of Madison Gas and Electric Company for Authority to Increase its Electric and Gas Rates.

13. *Ibid.*, p. 14.

14. *Ibid.*

15. *Ibid.*, p. 40-41, Commissioner Cudahy's discussion.

16. *Ibid.*, p. 47.

17. *Ibid.*, p. 48.

18. *Ibid.*, p. 49.

19. *Ibid.*

20. *Ibid.*, p. 50.

21. Critics of marginal cost pricing in general and peak load pricing in particular like to give the impression that there already exists a well-established and consistent set of principles on which electricity prices are currently based. Nothing could be further from the truth. Rather, there are at least 29 different costing and rate-making methodologies that have been used or suggested.

22. The famous French "Tarif Vert" is an industrial tariff, not a residential tariff. This fact was often lost in some of the early discussions. It is true, however, that in both England and France, optional time-of-day rates have been available to residential and commercial consumers for many years. See National Economic Research Associates, Inc. (1977).

23. This measure was emphasized by Cicchetti and by Nissel (1976). See Wenders and Taylor (1976) for a detailed discussion of the appropriate welfare calcualtions.

24. The lack of detailed point estimates need not delay implementation. We know that the demand functions have a negative slope from basic economic theory. We also know that the short-run responses are likely to be considerably smaller than the long-run response, making the possibility of rapid dramatic shifts in electrical load extremely unlikely. We also have information from the European experience. This information alone should allow us to embark on implementation for larger customers, fine-tuning the system as demand responses are "revealed" by implementation itself. Extensive implementation for residential consumers should probably proceed more cautiously. This is discussed further below.

25. This reflects a combination of regulatory accounting practice, increases in interest rates over embedded cost levels, and increases in the real costs of plant, rather than the result of "diseconomies of scale"; recent econometric studies still indicate that the industry is characterized by economies of scale as defined by economic theory (see Christiansen and Green, 1976), although some firms have gotten sufficiently large that most of the scale economies appear to have been exhausted.

26. Nissel (1964, 1969) provides an excellent example of this line of argument.

27. See *Electrical Week*, January 31, 1977, p. 7.

28. See *Electrical Week*, November 22, 1976, p. 2.

29. See *The Wall Street Journal*, March 31, 1977, p. 1.

30. See *Electrical Week*, December 22, 1976, p. 1-2.

31. See *Electrical Week*, January 31, 1977, p. 1.

32. See *Electrical Week*, December 27, 1976, p. 1-2.

33. See *Electrical Week*, March 28, 1977, p. 7.

34. It also appears to be the case that these commissions have an important "demonstration effect" on the commissions in other states.

35. The possibilities associated with remote metering through the use of the electrical lines as a vehicle for transmitting signals are very important. If these technologies perform as well as promised, they could reduce the metering

costs associated with both time-of-day rates and interruptible
rates considerably. An important impetus fostering these kinds
of technological advance is the expected demand for such
facilities. As more commissions act favorably on time-of-day
rates, demand expectations should increase considerably, with
an associated increase in research and development funds flowing
into this area.

REFERENCES CITED

Christensen, L. R., and Green, W. H. 1976, "Economies of scale
    in U.S. electric power generation." *Journal of Political
    Economy*, August.

Cicchetti, C., Testimony before the New York States Public
    Service Commission in Case No. 26806, Tr. 2691.

Clemens, 1963, "Marginal cost pricing: A comparison of French
    and American industrial power rates." *Land Economics*,
    October.

Joskow, P., 1974, "Inflation and environmental concern:
    Structural change in the process of public utility price
    requlation." *Journal of Law and Economics,* October.

Joskow, P., 1976, "Contributions to the theory of marginal cost
    pricing." *Bell Journal of Economics,* Spring.

Joskow, P., and MacAvoy, P., 1975, "Regulation and the financial
    performance of electric utilities in the 1970's."
    American Economic Review, May.

National Economic Research Associates, Inc., 1977, *Analysis of
    Electricity Pricing in France and Great Britain.*

Nelson, J., 1964, *Marginal Cost Pricing in Practice.* Englewood
    Cliffs, N.J., Prentice-Hall.

Nissel, H., 1969, "Incremental cost pricing and U.S. utility
    rates." *Public Utilities Fortnightly*, August 14.

Nissel, H., Testimony before the New York State Public Service
    Commission in Case No. 26806.

Nissel, H., 1976, "The electric rate question: Europe revisited"
    (synopsis). ELCON, November.

Pace, J., 1975, "The poor, the elderly and the rising cost of
    energy." *Public Utilities Fortnightly,* June 5.

Panzar, J. C., 1976, "A neoclassical approach to peak load pricing." *Bell Journal of Economics*, Autumn.

Shepherd, W. G., 1966, "Marginal cost pricing in American utilities." *Southern Economic Journal*, July.

Wenders, J. T., and Taylor, L. P., 1976, "Experiments in seasonal-time-of-day pricing of electricity to residential users." *Bell Journal of Economics*, Autumn.

2
Nonuniform Pricing Structures in Electricity

Roger W. Koenker
David S. Sibley

INTRODUCTION

In recent years, the literature on optimal pricing for
public utilities has been expanded to include nonuniform
pricing policies--that is, pricing schemes wherein the cost
of consuming a given amount of the utility's service is not
simply proportional to the amount consumed. Originating in
the two-part tariff literature (see Coase, 1946, and Feldstein, 1972), it has come to include optimal multipart tariffs
(see Faulhaber and Panzar, 1977) and, more generally, con-
tinuously varying nonuniform price schedules (see Spence,
1977, and Goldman, Leland, and Sibley, 1977).

Two characteristics of public utility economics have
given rise to this body of theory. First, utilities generally
face economies of scale,[1] so that uniform pricing at marginal
cost requires that the public enterprise be subsidized.
Second, consumers are diverse, and the planner has only
limited information about their demands. The two-part tariff
was originally conceived with the economy of scale problem
in mind: the usage charge would be set at marginal cost so as
to induce the Pareto-optimal amount of consumption, and the
entry fee would be set so as to bring the enterprise to a
break-even position. As long as the entry fee does not affect
the number of subscribers, the two-part tariff will achieve
the full welfare optimum.

However, if the entry fee exceeds surplus for some consumers at the marginal cost price, it reduces their welfare
to subscribe at all. Thus, although this two-part tariff is
nondistortionary with respect to the quantity decisions of the
participating consumer, it may distort the participation
decisions of other consumers. In the two-part tariff literature, several authors have examined this question, most notably
Littlechild (1975) and Ng and Weisser (1974).

This brings us to the second characteristic of public
utility cited above: limited information on the part of the
planner. If he had perfect information on the demand of each

consumer, he would engage in first-degree price discrimination.
As a practical matter the planner knows, at most, the distribution of demands across the population of consumers and thus
cannot engage in such price discrimination against individuals.
However, by offering a nonuniform price schedule and knowing
which points on the schedule will be selected by consumers of
different types, he can design the schedule to take advantage
of this information. Thus, he can achieve some of the effects
of price discrimination and design nonuniform price schedules
that are less distortionary than the two-part tariff.

In this chapter we apply the theory of nonuniform pricing
as developed in Goldman, Leland, and Sibley (1977) to the
case of residential pricing of electricity. We will ignore
peak load considerations for the most part and think of electric power as a single good irrespective of when it is consumed. At the end of the chapter we will briefly discuss
nonuniform prices in a peak load context. The whole effort is
exploratory and the results of our simulations should be
viewed as hypotheses for future research. Of course, much of
the interest of what we present will come from the insights
into nonlinear pricing that can be gleaned from numerical
analysis, as opposed to the theoretical nature of previous
work on nonuniform pricing.

For our purposes, we assume that the number of subscribers can be affected by pricing policies and, in particular,
that the two-part tariff is distortionary in this sense. How
much sense does this make in the case of residential electricity
demand? After all, it is hard to imagine a suburban homeowner
dropping off the distribution system of his local electric
utility, even at high levels of price and entry fee. At most,
he could switch to oil or natural gas for space and water
heating, but as a practical matter, it would be impossible
for him to cut electric power use to zero.

The answer depends partly on one's perspective.
Descending from the cosmic view taken here thus far, suppose
we are designing rate schedules for a particular utility in a
given geographic area. It is possible to imagine even a
suburban homeowner selling his all-electric home and moving
to an area served by another utility if electric rates became
too high. Also, a main feature of urban folklore is that
soaring costs of operating apartment buildings--including
electricity costs--cause widespread abandonment of apartment
houses in urban areas, particularly in areas such as New York
City, where rent control and urban blight are widespread.
Finally, in a dynamic sense, electric pricing policies in a
given area may discourage residential real estate construction.

The types of policies analyzed herein would almost certainly be appropriate for industrial customers, who can, and
often do, drop off the utility's distribution network and generate
their own electricity. Thus, many of the remarks made here
about the ways in which nonuniform prices operate will be of

24

interest to those who find unconvincing our argument for the plausibility of our assumption that two-part tariffs can affect the number of residential subscribers.

From this discussion, it would appear that some research effort should be devoted to the empirical demand for connection by customer class. Unfortunately, current econometric work on the demand for electricity does not address this question directly (see, for example, Taylor, 1975, and Taylor, Blattenberger, and Verleger, 1977). Instead, it focuses on income and price elasticities. To be sure, these questions have implications for the price elasticity of connection, but only if the elasticity estimates are assumed to be true globally, which strains credulity. In the absence of clear statistical evidence we will proceed on the assumption that the demand for connection is not perfectly inelastic.

THE WELFARE PRICING PROBLEM[2]

The first concern here is to set forth the pricing problem facing the planner and derive the optimal nonuniform price formula. This formula serves as the basis for the computational work undertaken further in the chapter.

The Planner

Consumers differ from each other according to a parameter, θ, which enters each consumer's willingess-to-pay function. We assume that income effects of the price changes contemplated herein are unimportant, so that willingness to pay for an additional unit of consumption is given by a function $\rho(q,\theta)$, where $\rho_q < 0$ and $\rho_\theta > 0$. If the value of θ for each consumer were known to the planner, the planner would design a separate price schedule for each consumer. However, since he does not have this knowledge, we assume that he knows the distribution of θ across the population. That is, he knows the density function $g(\theta)$, $\underline{\theta} \leq \theta \leq \overline{\theta}$, where

$$\int_{\underline{\theta}}^{\overline{\theta}} g(\theta)\,d\theta = 1 \qquad (1)$$

$$G(\theta) \equiv \int_{\underline{\theta}}^{\theta} g(v)\,dv, \quad G(\underline{\theta}) = 0, \quad G(\overline{\theta}) = 1 \qquad (2)$$

The planner knows the production costs, and we assume a constant marginal cost $c > 0$. He also operates subject to a revenue requirement constraint.

25

The planner's aim is to design an *outlay function, R(q)*, which gives the total amount a consumer must pay for consuming an amount q. We refer to the derivative $R'(q)$ as the "marginal price": It is the price of increasing consumption from q to $q + dq$. It will be convenient to denote the marginal price by $P(q)$. Knowing the reaction of different types of consumers to a given $R(q)$ or, equivalently, $P(q)$ schedule, the planner can design the schedule so as to maximize social welfare. First, however, let us analyze the reactions of different consumers to a given $P(q)$ schedule.

The Consumer

By assuming there is no importance of price-induced income effects, we imply that the consumer of type θ chooses his consumption so as to maximize net consumer surplus:

$$\max_{\{q\}} \left[\int_0^q \rho(s,\theta)\,ds - R(q) \right]. \tag{3}$$

His optimal consumer level, q^*, equates willingness to pay for an additional unit with the price for that additional unit:

$$\rho(q^*,\theta) = P(q^*) . \tag{4}$$

This procedure defines a function $q^*(\theta)$, given the optimal consumption of individual θ who faces a marginal price function $P(q)$.

Alternatively, we could pick a value of q and, given $P(q)$, determine which consumer group will find it optimal to consume just q and no more. That is, we could find a group $\hat{\theta}$ for whom willingness to pay is just equal to marginal price at q:

$$\rho(q,\hat{\theta}) = P(q) . \tag{5}$$

We refer to $\hat{\theta}$ as the "marginal consumer group" at q. Determination of $\hat{\theta}$ is depicted graphically in Figure 1a. In that diagram at $q = q_0$, $\hat{\theta}_0$ is the marginal consumer group. Consumers indexed by $\hat{\theta}_1 > \hat{\theta}_0$ have willingness to pay that exceeds marginal price at q_0 and will consume up to q_1. Consumers with $\theta < \hat{\theta}_0$ have willingness to pay that falls short of marginal price at q_0 and, therefore, will restrict their consumption to some smaller amount.

Equation (5) defines the marginal group at q as a function of marginal price at q. It is important to realize that $\hat{\theta}$ is an increasing function of $P(q)$ at a given q. This may be seen by totally differentiating equation (5):

$$\frac{\partial \hat{\theta}}{\partial P} = \frac{1}{\rho_\theta} > 0 \ . \tag{6}$$

This is true because, as we assumed above, demand is strictly increasing in θ. In Figure 1b we depict the situation graphically. Initially, at $q = q_0$, consumer group $\hat{\theta}_0$ is the marginal group. Now suppose it is displaced in a neighborhood that includes q_0; given the new price schedule, willingness to pay is less than the marginal price for group $\hat{\theta}_0$. Instead, a group with higher willingness to pay, $\hat{\hat{\theta}}_0 > \hat{\theta}_0$, is the new marginal consumer group at q_0. Group $\hat{\theta}_0$ now becomes the marginal consumer group at $\tilde{q} < q_0$.

Social Welfare Maximization

The planner chooses the function $P(q)$ to maximize aggregate consumer surplus plus profit. For a given consumption interval of width dq, total welfare is then:

$$F\big(q,P(q)\big)dq \equiv \int_{\theta^*(q)}^{\overline{\theta}} \Big\{ \big(\rho(q,\theta) - P(q)\big)$$

$$+ \big(P(q) - c\big) \Big\} g(\theta)\,d\theta\,dq \ , \tag{7}$$

where $\theta^*(q) \equiv \hat{\theta}\big(q,P(q)\big)$. Over the entire range of consumption, then, welfare is given by

$$\int_0^\infty F\big(q,P(q)\big)dq = \int_0^\infty \left[\int_{\theta^*(q)}^{\overline{\theta}} \Big\{ \big(\rho(q,\theta) - P(q)\big) \right.$$

$$\left. + \big(P(q) - c\big) \Big\} g(\theta)\,d\theta \right] dq \ . \tag{8}$$

A positive fixed cost $k > 0$ exists, so the marginal price function must satisfy the breakeven constraint:

$$\int_0^\infty \left[\int_{\theta^*(q)}^{\overline{\theta}} \big(P(q) - c\big)g(\theta)\,d\theta \right] dq = k \ . \tag{9}$$

27

Figure 1a

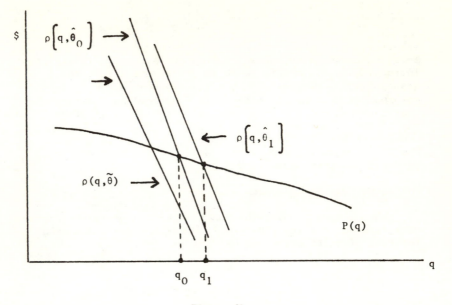

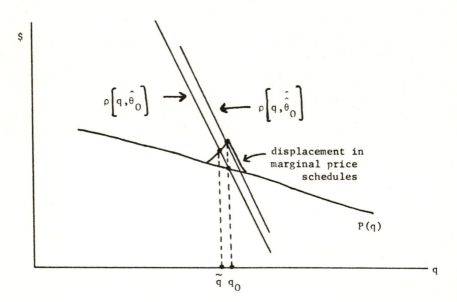

Figure 1b

The term inside square brackets in equation (9) is the contribution to profit of an interval of width dq.

Thus, the planner chooses $p(q)$ to maximize the following Lagrangean form:

$$\mathcal{L} = \int_0^\infty \left[\int_{\theta^*(q)}^{\overline{\theta}} \{ \left(\rho(q,\theta) - P(q) \right) + (1+\lambda) \cdot \left(P(q) - c \right) \} g(\theta) d\theta \right] dq - \lambda k,$$

(10)

where $\lambda \geq 0$ is the Lagrange multiplier for the profit constraint. Applying the calculus of variations to this problem, we obtain the following formula for the optimal marginal price function:

$$P(q) = c + \frac{\lambda}{1+\lambda} \cdot \frac{1 - G\left(\hat{\theta}(q)\right)}{g\left(\hat{\theta}_0(q)\right)} \cdot \frac{1}{\partial \hat{\theta}/\partial P} \cdot$$

(11)

We should note that for $\hat{\theta} < \overline{\theta}$, $P(q) > c$, and for $\theta = \overline{\theta}$, $P(q) = c$. Using this formula we compute optimal nonlinear price schedules using demand and cost data for residential electricity.

IMPLEMENTATION OF THE THEORY

From equation (11), it is evident that in order to compute price schedules we need to know marginal costs, overhead costs, and the function $\hat{\theta}\left(q, P(q)\right)$. Our treatment of cost is extremely casual; the work of Cicchetti, Gillen, and Smolensky (1976) suggests that a marginal operating cost of 2¢/kwh provides a reasonable basis for our exercise. In any event, the details of our story do not change much if this figure is allowed to vary. The level of overhead cost will be determined by the comparisons we make below, and whatever level of operating profit is achieved by the representative block rate schedules we have selected will be taken as the revenue requirement for the optimal nonuniform price.

To compute $\hat{\theta}\left(q, P(q)\right)$, we start by assuming that the willingness-to-pay function, $\rho(q,\theta)$, takes the Cobb-Douglas form:

$$\rho(q,\theta) = A \cdot q^{-1/\beta} \theta^\alpha$$

$$\gamma_0 = -\beta$$

(12)

where A, α, $\beta > 0$. The parameter θ will be interpreted as income from here on.[3] We take values of α and β from the

29

long-run income and price elasticities estimated in various econometric studies of the residential demand for electricity. For given values of α and β, we calibrate the demand function by choosing A so that at a marginal price of 2¢/kwh a consumer earning \$1,000 per month would consume 500 kwh per month. This seems a good average situation on which to base our analysis.

We will use the elasticity estimates arrived at by the Federal Energy Administration (FEA) and by Anderson (see Taylor, 1975), whose values of α, β, and A were

	α	β	A
FEA	1.1	-1.46	0.001
Anderson	0.8	-1.12	0.025

As far as θ is concerned, we assume a log normal distribution with a mean of \$1,000 per month (logarithmic mean and standard deviation of 6.9 and 1.0, respectively). We normalize the total population at unity.

For each run we compute the following: total social welfare, marginal price at each q, mean demand, mean expenditure, mean contribution to overhead, and the marginal consumer group at zero. Going back to our discussion of consumer behavior, the marginal consumer group at zero is the group that is just indifferent to either subscribing to the system or staying out. Its willingness to pay for an initial dq of consumption precisely equals the price of that first dq, which is the marginal price at zero. Symbolically, the marginal group at zero has an income $\theta^*(0)$ such that if $\rho\left(0, \theta^*(0)\right)$ exists, then

$$\rho\left(0, \theta^*(0)\right) = P(0) . \tag{13}$$

All those with incomes exceeding $\theta^*(0)$ consume positive amounts, and none of those with incomes less than $\theta^*(0)$ subscribe at all.

COMPUTATIONAL RESULTS

Profit Maximization

For conceptual simplicity we begin by analyzing the profit-maximizing price schedule. The formula for the optimal marginal price is obtained from equation (11) by letting $\lambda \to \infty$, so that we have

$$P(q) = c + \frac{1 - G\left(\hat{\theta}(q, P(q))\right)}{g\left(\hat{\theta}(q, P(q))\right)} \cdot \frac{1}{\dfrac{\partial \hat{\theta}}{\partial P(q)}} . \tag{14}$$

30

Figure 2

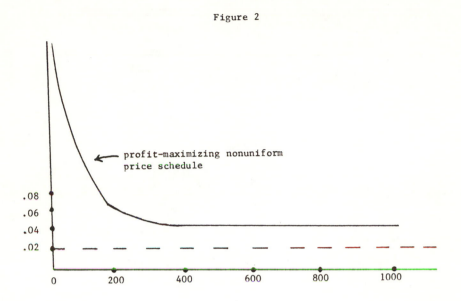

In this case, the economic problem is to design a price
schedule that extracts considerable consumer surplus from the
high demanders (in this case, the high-income consumers) without forcing them out of the market or curtailing their demand
too much. This may be done even at the cost of forcing many
low- to moderate-income consumers off the system.

In Figure 2 we depict the profit-maximizing nonuniform
price schedule, which displays quantity discounts in the form
of declining marginal prices. The schedule appears to work in
two ways. First, it charges high marginal prices for the
first few kilowatt hours, where aggregate demand is most inelastic. Second, the quantity discounts that persist throughout act as inducements to consume in the face of high *levels*
of marginal price; that is, they reduce the deadweight loss of
high marginal prices.

Specifically, Table 1 gives the marginal prices at
selected consumption levels. Note that the marginal price at
0.1 kwh is extremely high by comparison to the entry fees on
most block rate tariffs currently in use[4]; of course, it only
applies to an infinitesimal amount dq. By 100 kwh, the
marginal price has fallen by a factor of 90, but remains well
above the 2¢ marginal cost for all reasonable ranges of consumption. Recall from equation (11) that $P(q)$ must approach
2¢ asymptotically.

TABLE 1. MARGINAL PRICES AT SELECTED
CONSUMPTION LEVELS

Quantity (kwh/month)	Marginal price ($)
0.1	7.34
1.0	1.53
100	0.084
200	0.061
300	0.051
400	0.046
500	0.043
..	..
..	..
..	..
1,500	0.033
..	..
..	..
..	..
4,000	0.028

The overall effects of this price schedule are:

        social welfare   = $21.5
        profit   = $15.61
        marginal group at zero = $924.50
        mean demand[5]   = 288 kwh/month.

Once again, social welfare is herein considered the sum of
total consumer surplus and profit, so that either (1) dis-
tributional considerations are unimportant, or (2) they are
being satisfied by an income tax system exogenous to our
problem. The most noteworthy result now is that roughly one-
half of the population of consumers is being priced out of
the market under this scheme; the emphasis is on finding a
price schedule that will "price-discriminate" effectively
against high income users.

    Let us compare the social effects of the profit-maximizing
nonuniform price schedule with those of the profit-maximizing

32

TABLE 2. MARGINAL PRICES FOR CONSUMPTION
LEVELS IN THE FIRST KWH

kwh	Marginal price ($)
0.1	7.34
0.2	4.57
0.3	3.47
0.4	2.85
0.5	2.45
0.6	2.17
0.7	1.95
0.8	1.78
0.9	1.64
1.0	1.53

uniform price. The latter turns out to be 6.85¢/kwh and performs as follows:

social welfare   = $17.08

profit   = $8.53

average consumption = 175.96 kwh/month.

At this price, virtually no consumers are being priced out of
the market. Evidently, the nonuniform price is a much better
profit incentive, having the flexibility to price low surplus
consumers out of the market and then extract surplus from the
high demanders, using quantity discounts to minimize deadweight loss. This is a striking instance of how nonuniform
prices act as partial price discriminators.

For further insight into how nonuniform price schedules
work, Table 2 shows the marginal prices for consumption levels
in the first kilowatt hour. The magnitudes of marginal price
in this range suggest that the first few kilowatt hours contribute greatly to the overall level of profit. In fact, the
first kilowatt hour contributes $1.30 of profit--not an in-
considerable amount--out of the total $15.61. The first 100
kwh contribute $9.63. This suggests that when welfare
maximization is considered, whatever level of operating profit
is required will be made up by marginal prices in the lower
ranges of consumption; marginal price in the middle and upper

ranges of consumption will be set close to marginal cost.

Welfare Maximization

In this section we compare the welfare attainable from a
nonuniform price schedule of the form of equation (11) with
that attainable by representative block rate tariffs. We
selected these tariffs from the *National Electric Rate Book*
(1976) more or less at random and computed the social welfare
attained by these tariffs given the following: (1) a marginal
cost of 2¢/kwh and (2) the demand specifications of Anderson
and the FEA noted above. We then compute the social welfare
attained by the optimal nonuniform price schedule when the
latter is constrained to yield the same level of operating
profit as did the block schedule to which it is being compared.
First, we consider the following block tariff[6]:

$$\text{fixed charge} = \$1.20$$

$$\text{marginal price} = \$0.0418, \; q \leq 100$$

$$= \$0.0314, \; q > 100.$$

With the FEA elasticities, this block tariff performs as
follows:

social welfare	= $16.57
mean demand	= 490 kwh/month
mean expenditure	= $17.28
operating profit	= $7.50
marginal consumer group at zero	= $338.25

As a quick check on the realism of our demand specification,
the monthly demand and expenditure figures seem reasonable.
The fixed charge of $1.20 forces consumers with incomes of
less than $338.25 out of the market. That is, their net
surplus is less than $1.20.

Now we compute the nonuniform price schedule which
maximizes social welfare when operating profits must equal
$7.50. In Figure 3 are depicted the nonuniform price and the
block rate tariff. As expected, marginal price under the
optimal schedule considerably exceeds that under the block rate
for the first few kilowatt hours and then falls below the block
tariff at middle ranges of consumption. The social results of
the optimal nonuniform price schedule are:

social welfare	= $25.82
mean demand	= 664.73 kwh/month
mean expenditure	= $20.75
operating profit	= $7.50
marginal consumer group at zero	= $247.45.

Figure 3

A Comparison of Block and Welfare Optimal Tariffs

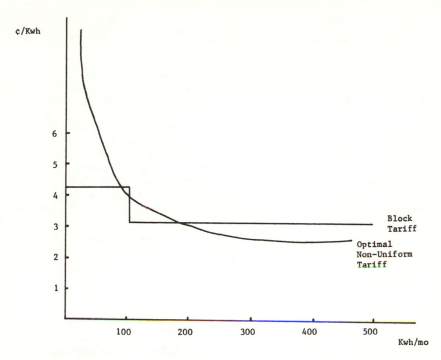

The optimal schedule, then, achieves about 60 percent greater welfare than does the block tariff. It does so by raising marginal prices in the first few kilowatt hours to meet the $7.50 revenue requirement and by setting the marginal price much closer to marginal cost than under the block rate, so that more consumers buy at or close to their Pareto-optimal levels. Because the charge for the initial kilowatt hour is more usage-sensitive under the optimal schedule than under the block rate, fewer consumers leave the system, the marginal group at zero being $247.45 instead of $338.25.

Using the FEA elasticities, we can compare the optimal schedule to a more elaborate block rate schedule[7]:

$$
\begin{aligned}
\text{fixed charge} \quad &= \$1.50 \\
\text{marginal price} \quad &= \$0.046, \ 0 \le q \le 150 \\
&= \$0.035, \ 151 \le q \le 400 \\
&= \$0.032, \ 401 \le q \le 1{,}000 \\
&= \$0.030, \ 1{,}001 \le q.
\end{aligned}
$$

The difference here is even more dramatic:

	Block rate	Optimal schedule
social welfare	$12.98	$24.8
operating profit	$5.8	$5.8

In making the same comparisons using the Anderson elasticities, the total surplus (= consumer surplus plus profit) is smaller, because both price and income elasticities are smaller (1.12 versus 1.46, 0.8 versus 1.1) and because of the way the constant term in the demand equation is chosen. We might thus expect that equation (10), though superior to the block rate schedules, will be less markedly so because the potential payoff to optimal pricing, in terms of better extraction of surplus, is more limited. Using the first block schedule as a basis for comparison, we see that this is the case:

	Block rate	Optimal schedule
social welfare	$38.58	$46.00
operating profit	$4.56	$4.56

CONCLUSIONS

Because this study was exploratory in nature, we have no conclusions--only hypotheses for future research. We hope to have suggested that substantial welfare gains may result from the use of nonuniform pricing theory. The principal means by which the optimal schedules analyzed here have dominated the block rate tariffs have been (1) much higher marginal prices in the first few kilowatt hours of electricity consumption so as to generate the required level of profit and (2) lower marginal prices for middle and higher ranges of consumption so as to set the consumption levels of individuals who are not priced out of the market closer to the Pareto-efficient levels. Also, because a consumer's outlay in low levels of q is more usage-sensitive than under the block rate tariffs with their fixed entry fees, fewer consumers are priced out of the market.

To investigate the gains from optimal rate structure more carefully, however, requires not only more detailed work of the sort undertaken here, but econometric demand analysis of a kind somewhat different from that currently engaged in by most researchers. A crucial empirical question from the standpoint of pricing theory is whether subscribers will drop off the system as a result of the pricing policies undertaken by the regulated firm. If they are unlikely to drop off, then the two-part tariff is the optimal pricing structure. If they do, then nonuniform pricing policies of the sort analyzed here will be optimal. Current empirical work does not address this issue. Instead, it focuses on estimates of long-run and short-run price and income elasticities. Although these parameters imply something about the demand for connections to the system, few would be so bold as to insist that they hold true for ranges of consumption far away from the mean. The need is for explicit consideration of the decision to connect to or drop off the system. In the case of industrial demand--for which analysis similar to this work could easily be done--this is likely to be particularly important because of customer firms' abilities to self-generate. A second and related research priority is to study the willingness of consumers who do subscribe to pay for the first few kilowatt hours; the usefulness of nonuniform pricing depends critically on careful exploitation of demand for the initial amounts of consumption.

Another point of interest brought out by our analysis is that the optimality of quantity discounts need not depend on declining marginal costs, as is sometimes argued. The fundamental motivation for having quantity discounts is that of achieving some sorting of heterogeneous customers.

One final concern is how nonuniform pricing fits into the current movement toward peak load pricing. Presumably the two should be integrated--that is, one nonuniform price schedule might obtain in the off-peak period and another during the peak period. For example, if technology is in fixed proportion with the marginal operating cost c and marginal capacity cost β, constant returns prevail. Suppose the setup of the problem is the same as presented here, except that there are two time periods with independent demands $\rho^1(q^1,\theta)$ and $\rho^2(q^2,\theta)$ with $\rho^2 > \rho^1$ for all q and θ. If we maximize the sum of social welfares across the periods, the optimal peak-load prices would be

$$P^1(q^1) = c + \frac{\lambda}{1+\lambda} \cdot \left[\frac{1 - G(\hat{\theta}^1)}{g(\hat{\theta}^1) \; \frac{\partial \theta^1}{\partial P}} \right]$$

$$P^2(q^2) = c + \beta + \left[\frac{1 - G(\hat{\theta}^2)}{g(\hat{\theta}^2) \; \frac{\partial \hat{\theta}^2}{\partial P^2}} \right] \cdot \left[\frac{\lambda}{1+\lambda} \right] \cdot$$

Thus, the general sort of analysis undertaken here extends into problems of peak-load pricing as well. The peak users should face a nonuniform pricing scheme like equation (10). Again, this assumes that the demand for connection to the system has some elasticity.

NOTES

1. By "economics of scale" we refer to the standard economics notion of increases in output requiring less than proportionate increases in inputs, with factor prices constant. In public forums, this notion is often confused with divergences between marginal costs (at current prices) and average embedded costs. These imperfections of inflation accounting are irrelevant to our exercise.

2. The entire analysis in this section is drawn from Goldman, Leland, and Sibley (1977).

3. In using consumer surplus we are not assuming that income has no effect on the demand for electricity, but that the income effects of all price changes are small.

4. See the *National Electric Rate Book* (1976).

5. Recall that population is set at unity so that total demand

$$\int_0^\infty \left\{ 1 - G\left(\hat{\theta}(q, P(q)) \right) \right\} dq$$

has the interpretation of a mean.

6. This block tariff is the residential tariff used by Commonwealth Edison Company (*National Electric Rate Book,* 1976).

7. This block schedule is the one used by the Los Angeles Department of Water and Power (Acton, Mitchell, and Mowill, 1976).

REFERENCES CITED

Acton, J., Mitchell, B., and Mowill, R., 1976, *Residential Demand for Electricity in Los Angeles: An Econometric Study Using Disaggregated Data.* Rand, September.

Cicchetti, C. J., Gillen, W. J., and Smolensky, P., 1976, *The Marginal Cost and Pricing of Electricity: An Applied Approach.* Planning and Conservation Foundation, Sacramento, June.

Coase, R. H., 1946, "The marginal cost controversy." *Economica,* Vol. 13.

Faulhaber, G. R., and Panzar, J. C., 1977, "Optimal two-part tariffs with self-selection." Bell Laboratories Economics Discussion Paper No. 74, January.

Feldstein, M., 1972, "Equity and efficiency in public sector pricing: The optimal two-part tariff." *Quarterly Journal of Economics*, May.

Goldman, M. B., Leland, H. E., and Sibley, D. S., 1977, "Optimal nonuniform pricing." Bell Laboratories Economics Discussion Paper No. 100, May.

Littlechild, S. C., 1975, "Two-part tariffs and consumption externalities." *Bell Journal of Economics and Management Science*, Autumn.

National Electric Rate Book, 1976, Federal Power Commission, United States Government Printing Office, May.

Ng, Y., and Weisser, M., 1974, "Optimal pricing with a budget constraint: The case of the two-part tariff." *Review of Economic Studies*, July.

Spence, A. M., 1977, "Nonlinear prices and welfare." *Journal of Public Economics*, Vol. 8, no. 1, p. 1-18.

Taylor, L., 1975, "The demand for electricity: A survey." *Bell Journal of Economics and Management Science*, Spring.

Taylor, L., Blattenberger, G., and Verleger, P., 1977, *The Residential Demand for Energy*. Electric Power Research Institute, January.

3
Natural Gas Regulations: Problems and Options

Lawrence Kumins

THE CURRENT SITUATION AND HOW IT DEVELOPED

The 1938 Natural Gas Act[1] granted the Federal Power Commission (FPC) power to regulate interstate sales of natural gas for resale. In its initial interpretation, the Gas Act appeared to mean that the FPC would control the charges of interstate pipeline firms selling gas to distribution companies. Only the pipeline firms' tariffs for transporting gas were regulated; wellhead prices paid to producers were, in this early interpretation, excluded by Section I(b), which states "The provisions of this Act . . . shall not apply . . . to the production or gathering of natural gas."

Mainline direct sales to end users of interstate pipelines were also excluded, and they remain outside FPC purview today. Most local distribution of natural gas is an intrastate activity and falls under the jurisdiction of state public utility commissions.

A piece of New Deal legislation, the Natural Gas Act's goal was to insure that consumers paid "fair" prices for gas sold by an industry that was just beginning to develop at that time. Wellhead prices were extremely low then because of the Depression and the fact that the interstate pipeline system was in its infancy. In many producing areas, monopsonistic situations existed, in which single pipeline buyers were able to dictate field prices.

Viewed in retrospect, there are two interpretations of the language that governs the scope of the Gas Act:

1. The market forces working at that time were sufficient to maintain fair prices to users, and Congress actually intended field prices to be unregulated.

The views contained herein are solely the author's and should not be construed to represent views of the Library of Congress, other members of the Library staff, or any member of Congress.

41

2. Section I(b) contained an inadequate definition of
where interstate commerce began. Was this language
intended to include the gathering and production
of gas sold in interstate commerce and to exclude
sales for intrastate use, or was it designed to
exclude all production and gathering?

The FPC held that Section I(b) meant that its jurisdiction
did not extend to production and gathering.

This arrangement continued until 1954, when the Supreme
Court ruled in the Phillips case that the FPC indeed had
regulatory responsibility for production and gathering.[2] The
case arose out of a dispute between Phillips Petroleum, the
Wisconsin Public Service Commission (PSC), and the Detroit
Corporation Counsel. Phillips had signed a contract in 1945
with the Michigan-Wisconsin Pipeline to deliver gas for 5¢ per
thousand cubic feet (Mcf). The contract was renegotiated in
1949 to 8.5¢. At that time, the contract's inflation adjustment factor was changed so that the price paid to Phillips was
tied to the city gate price received by Michigan-Wisconsin.
On the basis of complaints by Detroit and the Wisconsin PSC,
the FPC scheduled hearings inquiring into the rate's reasonable-
ness. However, the agenda was changed to determine only the
question of the FPC's jurisdiction.[3] The Commission refused to
take jurisdiction, and the Wisconsin PSC brought suit in the
District of Columbia Court of Appeals. In May 1953, the Court
reversed the FPC ruling. The Supreme Court heard the appeal
and upheld the finding that Phillips was indeed a natural gas
company within the Gas Act's intent and that its sales in
interstate commerce were indeed subject to FPC jurisdiction.

Thereafter, the FPC began to regulate wellhead prices
on a producer-by-producer basis. Their initial efforts were
rather half-hearted, because Congressional action relieving
this court-imposed mandate was anticipated. Congress did pass
the Harris-Fulbright Act in 1956, which would have deregulated
gas, but it was vetoed by President Eisenhower. The President,
while agreeing with the principles, felt compelled to veto because of "arrogant lobbying" for its passage[4] and allegations
that producers were buying votes. While other attempts at
removing the producer regulation were made, none reached the
House floor.

The FPC began to apply the same regulatory format used in
electric utility and gas pipeline rate making. In practice,
only eleven full-scale producer rate cases were heard during
the 1954-1960 period. All except one (which was never concluded) showed producers' revenues to be less than costs.
Within the pricing guidelines established by these proceedings,
however, the FPC accepted about 11,000 rate schedules from
3,372 independent producers between 1954 and 1960.[5] About
33,000 supplements to these schedules had been filed by 1960,
and a substantial backlog of cases existed in which rates had
been suspended pending hearings.

42

Owing to the hearing backlog and because of the futility of setting rates that were often above contract prices, the Commission switched its regulatory format away from the individual producer concept to a broader basis--the geologically homogeneous producing area. Not only would this consolidate backlogged rate cases, but it would determine fair gas prices based on financial requirements of broad industry segments rather than an individual firm's cost of service. In 1961, the FPC held the Permian Basin Area hearing, the first of its kind. This proceeding was culminated in 1965, when the Commission chose 16.5¢/Mcf as the appropriate area rate (Opinion 468). A lower price was set for old gas contracted for sale in the interstate market before 1961, thus establishing a multitiered pricing system based on gas vintage. Other area rates were subsequently set, and during the late 1960s and early 1970s, rates for gas from new wells in the various areas were increased.

Problems stemming from a complex set of different rates for the various producing areas and vintages led the FPC in 1974 to attempt simplification by abandoning the area rate concept in favor of a single nationwide rate. Opinion 699 set this at 42¢/Mcf for "new" gas from wells started or gas sold for the first time in interstate commerce after January 1, 1973. The 1973-1974 vintage rate was subsequently adjusted to 50¢/Mcf for the period after January 1, 1975.

On July 27, 1976, the FPC issued Opinion 770, which set a new and radically higher national rate of $1.42/Mcf for new gas developed after January 1, 1975. The 1973-1974 rate was increased from 52¢ to 93¢/Mcf (as modified by Opinion 770A in November 1976), and older gas from expiring contracts was allowed to be continued in interstate commerce at 52¢. All rates are subject to adjustments for Btu content, state severance tax reimbursement, and gathering allowances.

What actually happened to average gas prices under the various rate-making approaches can be evaluated by examining the path of average current and constant-dollar prices paid to producers over time (Table 1). One can see from the table that the period of individual producer regulation was generally characterized by rising wellhead prices. By 1961, as the area rate approach began to replace producer regulation, prices--especially in real terms--began to decline, as did real (unregulated) oil prices. This decline continued throughout the 1960s.

Production Trends

During this period, the gas pipeline industry was growing rapidly. Miles of pipeline and main doubled after the Phillips decision: revenues increased from $3.5 billion in 1954 to $19.1 billion in 1975; sales rose from 6.7 trillion cubic feet (Tcf) annually to a 1972 high of 17.1 Tcf.

Against this backdrop of a seemingly healthy and rapidly

TABLE 1. NEW GAS CONTRACT PRICES, 1953-1969

Year	New interstate contract price (¢/Mcf)	New contract price in 1958 dollars
1953	13.3	15.1
1954	11.7	13.1
1955	14.4	15.8
1956	14.8	15.7
1957	16.9	17.3
1958	18.6	18.6
1959	18.4	18.1
1960	18.2	17.6
1961	17.9	17.1
1962	17.5	16.5
1963	17.0	15.9
1964	16.2	14.9
1965	17.4	15.7
1966	17.4	15.3
1967	18.6	15.8
1968	19.0	15.5
1969	19.7	15.4

Source: Patricia E. Starratt and Robert M. Spann, 1974, "Alternative strategies for dealing with the natural gas shortage in the United States." In Edward W. Erickson and Leonard Waverman, eds., The Energy Question: An International Failure of Policy, Vol. 2, "North America," University of Toronto Press, Toronto and Buffalo, p. 31.

expanding industry, the reported gas supply underpinning the apparent growth was beginning to diminish. Proven natural gas reserves in the lower 48 states peaked in 1967, and in 1968 production exceeded new discoveries for the first time. Reserve additions in the lower 48 states have never equalled annual consumption again, even though production continued to rise until 1972. As Table 2 indicates, reported reserve additions were, relative to consumption, high from 1954 to 1967, even though real prices declined during about the last half of that period. Production from the declining reserve base peaked in 1973 and has declined significantly since that time.

TABLE 2. NATURAL GAS PRODUCTION COMPARED TO DISCOVERIES,
REVISIONS, AND EXTENSIONS OF PROVEN GAS RESERVES,
1950-1975 (Tcf)

Year	Discoveries, revisions, extensions	Net production
1950	12.0	6.9
1951	16.0	7.9
1952	14.3	8.6
1953	20.3	9.2
1954	9.5	9.4
1955	21.9	10.1
1956	24.7	10.8
1957	20.0	11.4
1958	18.9	11.4
1959	20.6	12.4
1960	13.9	13.0
1961	17.2	13.4
1962	19.5	13.6
1963	18.2	14.5
1964	20.3	15.3
1965	21.3	16.3
1966	20.2	17.5
1967	21.8	18.4
1968	13.7	19.4
1969	8.4	20.7
1970	37.2*	22.0
1971	9.8	22.1
1972	9.6	22.5
1973	6.8	22.6
1974	8.7	21.3
1975	10.5	19.7

*Includes Alaska.
Source: American Gas Association, 1976, Gas Facts, Table 4, p. 12.

REGULATORY PERFORMANCE

The 1954-1973 Experience

It is difficult to evaluate whether or not the FPC did the correct thing in regulating wellhead prices. Critics assert that utility-type regulation was inappropriate for the gas-producing industry, because producing firms were highly competitive. Those favoring regulation have held, as did the Supreme Court, that it was necessary to assure fair prices to consumers. The following points can be made describing regulatory experience prior to the generalized rise in energy prices following the Arab Oil Embargo.

1. During the initial six years, it would appear that FPC regulation did not lower prices appreciably. Indeed, in its early years, the FPC's court-imposed role in field markets may have diminished the monopsonistic power exercised by some pipelines in some of the major producing areas, resulting in prices higher than would have occurred otherwise, had the FPC not set producer prices above monopsony levels.

2. At some time between 1962 and 1968, the perceived demand for gas probably reached a level sufficiently greater than supply at burner-tip prices below those of oil fuels for wellhead gas prices to have converged on Btu equivalence with oil. This would have meant that industrial users, who consume half of the gas sold by utilities--and are the first to switch fuels on the basis of relative prices--would have bid the price up to the equivalent of oil fuel prices. During each of these years, industrial sales averaged 35¢/Mcf, of which about 20¢ was for transport and distribution; wellhead prices averaged less than 15¢/Mcf (or per million Btus). During this period, industrial bulk fuel users could purchase distillate fuel oil at 15¢/gallon or roughly $1.00 per million Btus.[6] Residual fuel averaged $4.00/barrel, or about 70¢/million Btus. Given these oil fuel price levels, the potential existed at some point during this period for burner-tip gas prices to rise from 35¢ to between 70¢ and $1.00. Wellhead prices, therefore, could have risen 50¢ to 80¢ from an average of 15¢, except where contracts between producers and pipelines prohibited increases.

It is difficult to speculate how, in the absence of regulation, contracts signed in the 1940s and 1950s would have been honored as excess supplies disappeared. No doubt many would have been broken or renegotiated. This price boost of 35¢ to 70¢, if applied to all flowing gas during the 1960s,

46

could have cost consumers between $6.7 and $12.0 billion yearly during the latter 1960s. These figures represent savings that accrued to both intrastate and interstate gas users, inasmuch as interstate prices tended to set intrastate ceilings during much of the 1960s.

The Post-Oil Embargo Experience

Production first exceeded discoveries in 1968, and this trend continued to increase until 1973. It declined to 21.3 Tcf in 1974, 19.7 Tcf in 1975, and an estimated 19.6 Tcf in 1976. Meanwhile, both potential and actual demand continued to grow, even though an unintended form of allocation came into play in the form of an inability by distribution systems and pipelines to add customers and later through formal curtailment of existing users. While Table 2 shows the time path of production, Table 3 shows the growth of actual curtailments of firm service by interstate pipelines due to inadequate gas production, largely during peak winter months.

Against this increasingly visible shortfall, both interstate and intrastate prices began to rise. While no data are available on intrastate prices until the beginning of 1975, interstate prices have risen and doubled since the Arab Oil Embargo of 1973-1974. Although the facts are not entirely clear, intrastate prices were generally conceded to be around the 50¢/Mcf level prior to the Embargo--near Btu parity with industrial oil fuels. Three years after the Embargo, average

TABLE 3. NET CURTAILMENTS OF CONTRACTUALLY FIRM INTERSTATE GAS DELIVERIES, 1972-1977

Period	Billion cubic feet
9/72-8/73	1,031
4/73-3/74	1,191
9/73-8/74	1,362
4/74-3/75	2,013
9/74-8/75	2,418
9/75-8/76	2,976
4/76-3/77	3,338
9/76-8/77	3,771

Source: Federal Power Commission.

interstate prices just began reaching pre-Embargo intrastate levels. Intrastate gas, in turn, escalated to an average of $1.85/Mcf.

Post-Embargo Pricing Situation

After the Embargo and its associated price increases for oil and intrastate gas, the FPC issued in June 1974 the first national rate of 42¢/Mcf in Opinion 699, which applied only to gas produced from wells drilled on or after January 1, 1973. An inflation adjustment of 1¢/Mcf per year was provided for, as well as Btu content, state severance tax, and gathering cost allowances. This rate was promulgated in the summer of 1974 and affected prices retroactively. Gas sold between January 1, 1973, and the time of Opinion 699 had been placed in interstate commerce at pre-existing area rates. After Opinion 699, producers could apply for the new rate for eligible gas. It was not until late 1974 that higher prices became noticeable in the average or "blend" price by pipelines. In Opinion 699H, issued in December 1974, maximum rates were raised to 50¢/Mcf plus adjustments (52¢/Mcf with the inflation adjustment), and blend prices continued to rise. When the FPC raised rates to $1.42/Mcf plus adjustments in Opinion 770, average prices paid by interstate pipelines rose at an accelerated rate.[7]
Interstate prices, now averaging nearly 60¢/Mcf, will converge in time to the $1.42 rate (plus adjustments). How long this convergence will take is hard to estimate. However, between January 1973 (to which Opinion 699 rates were applicable) and August 1976 (when producers actually could file for Opinion 770 rates), prices rose by 133 percent from 24¢/Mcf to 56¢/Mcf. During the one and one-half years between the announcement of the 42¢ ceiling and the next increase to 52¢, producers had been able to increase average prices up to the then-current new gas ceilings. With constant readjustments of old rates, which the FPC has provided for in Opinions 699H, 770, and 770A and other ad hoc measures aimed at increasing prices, substantial price rises already are programmed into the system. Without any changes in regulatory procedure or new increases in the FPC's national ceilings, it appears that average interstate prices will converge on the $1.50/Mcf level in four or five years. This will cost gas users over $10 billion per year more than they now pay for today's volume of gas deliveries. The fact that large price increases are already programmed for all classes of interstate gas consumers, even before Congressional action on the National Energy Act, should not be overlooked.

Intrastate Prices

To a large extent, intrastate gas markets have been protected from nationwide demand by regulation of interstate

TABLE 4. RECENT INTRASTATE WELLHEAD GAS PRICES
(dollars/Mcf)

	New contracts			Renegotiated or amended contracts		
	High	Weighted average	Low	High	Weighted average	Low
1975 average	2.07	1.29	0.43	2.13	1.42	0.26
January	2.00	1.12	0.49	2.17	1.44	0.21
February	1.95	1.20	0.43	2.07	1.49	0.76
March	2.07	1.04	0.56	2.08	0.76	0.25
April	2.04	1.54	0.20	1.91	1.67	0.25
May	2.04	1.42	0.44	2.08	1.46	0.19
June	2.12	1.20	0.47	2.32	1.58	0.20
July	2.08	1.48	0.31	2.35	1.52	0.26
August	2.20	1.36	0.30	2.17	1.06	0.44
September	2.14	1.42	0.40	2.12	1.53	0.25
October	2.03	1.05	0.38	2.11	1.51	0.13
November	1.94	1.36	0.46	2.04	1.74	0.37
December	2.16	1.34	0.75	2.09	1.32	0.38
1976 average	2.08	1.61	0.49	2.19	1.64	0.49
January	2.00	1.55	0.14	2.21	1.84	0.25
February	2.13	1.62	0.15	2.21	1.70	0.26
March	1.90	1.52	0.71	2.21	1.62	0.45
April	2.16	1.73	0.51	2.09	1.22	0.18
May	2.01	1.39	0.15	2.34	1.83	0.16
June	2.04	1.67	0.29	2.18	1.71	0.49
July	2.17	1.27	0.49	2.21	1.15	0.20
August	2.03	1.55	0.40	2.29	1.69	0.80
September	1.97	1.72	0.93	2.28	1.95	0.97
October	2.12	1.79	0.47	2.16	1.58	0.48
November	2.09	1.65	1.16	1.99	1.63	0.50
December	2.33	1.85	0.46	2.17	1.76	1.14
1977						
January	2.35	1.81	0.19	2.31	1.85	0.82
February	1.98	1.66	0.42	2.31	1.76	0.45
March	2.39	1.91	0.44	2.35	1.71	0.34

Source: FPC, Bureau of Natural Gas, 1975-1976, "Intrastate gas prices of FPC jurisdictional natural gas companies selling more than one million Mcf. per year in interstate commerce." FPC Form 45.

prices. States with large amounts of gas production--notably Texas and Louisiana--have found large supplies available to meet the demands of their home markets. Interstate price regulation has been responsible for depressed prices in these states for at least a decade. These artificially low prices represent an often unmeasured, indirect benefit of FPC regulation to intrastate consumers. While significant protection still exists, the impact of Opinion 770 on prices in the western South-Central states is becoming observable. Table 4 shows how prices in new and renegotiated intrastate contracts have increased since the FPC began collecting data.

In Table 5 are shown the prices paid by electric utilities in the western South-Central states during roughly the same period. These data encompass prices in large transactions under old contracts and are likely to be indicative of average intrastate wholesale prices. While these prices include some interstate gas as well as relatively small transport charges, their escalation in the post-Embargo era clearly charts the upward trend in intrastate prices for already flowing (old) gas.

TABLE 5. GAS PRICES PAID BY ELECTRIC UTILITIES IN TEXAS, LOUISIANA, OKLAHOMA, AND KANSAS, YEAR END

Year	Price (¢/Mcf)
1972	27
1973	34
1974	54
1975	83
1976	100

Source: FPC Form 423.

Emergency Natural Gas Act of 1977

Shortly after assuming office, President Carter proposed legislation that addressed the unexpectedly severe gas curtailments of the winter of 1976-1977. The bill, which was passed virtually unamended, contained two major provisions, which permitted (1) the allocation of gas among interstate pipelines until April 30, 1977, and (2) purchases from both intrastate producers and pipelines at prices that "the President determines to be appropriate." Under this law, the FPC authorized less than 50 billion cubic feet of emergency sales at prices averaging $2.25/Mcf.

Trends in Drilling

Table 6 delineates the trend in drilling activity during the past quarter century. Its highlight is the upsurge in gas wells drilled since 1974. Moreover, 1976 was a record year for gas well completions.

TABLE 6. DRILLING ACTIVITY IN THE UNITED STATES

| Year | Total well completions | | | | | Total feet drilled* |
	Oil	Gas	Dry	Service	Total	
1957	28,612	4,626	20,983	1,409	55,024	233.1
1958	24,578	4,803	19,043	1,615	50,039	198.2
1959	25,800	5,029	19,265	1,670	51,764	209.2
1960	21,186	5,258	17,574	2,733	46,751	190.7
1961	21,101	5,664	17,106	3,091	46,962	192.1
1962	21,249	5,848	16,682	2,400	46,179	198.6
1963	20,288	4,751	16,347	2,267	43,653	184.4
1964	20,620	4,855	17,488	2,273	45,236	189.9
1965	18,761	4,724	16,025	1,922	41,432	181.5
1966	16,780	4,377	15,227	1,497	37,881	166.0
1967	15,329	3,659	13,246	1,584	33,818	144.7
1968	14,331	3,456	12,812	2,315	32,914	149.3
1969	14,368	4,083	13,736	1,866	34,053	160.9
1970	13,020	3,840	11,260	1,347	29,467	142.4
1971	11,858	3,830	10,163	1,449	27,300	128.3
1972	11,306	4,928	11,057	1,464	28,755	138.4
1973	9,902	6,385	10,305	1,010	27,602	138.9
1974	12,784	7,240	11,674	1,195	32,893	153.8
1975	16,408	7,580	13,247	1,862	39,097	178.5
1976	17,059	9,085	13,621	1,690	41,455	185.3

*In millions of feet.
Source: Independent Petroleum Association of America.

Year	Revisions	Extensions	New field discoveries	New reservoir discoveries in old fields
			Changes in reserves during year	
1965	14,775,570†		6,543,709†	
1966	4,937,962	9,224,745	2,947,329	3,110,396
1967	6,570,578	9,538,584	3,170,520	2,524,651
1968	3,016,146	7,758,821	1,376,429	1,545,612
1969	(1,238,261)	5,800,489	1,769,557	2,043,219
1970	(99,721)	6,158,168	27,770,223	3,367,689
1971	(1,227,400)	6,374,706	1,317,574	3,360,541
1972	(1,077,791)	6,153,683	1,462,539	3,096,132
1973	(3,474,756)	6,177,286	2,152,151	1,970,368
1974	(1,333,285)	5,847,251	2,013,745	2,151,473
1975	383,449	6,027,433	2,423,382	1,649,424
1976	(1,197,119)	5,337,707	1,421,013	1,993,867

*Preliminary net production.
†Separation of revisions from extensions of new field discoveries from new reservoir discoveries in old fields not available prior to 1966.

One can speculate on the reasons why the number of gas wells increased so rapidly between 1972 and 1976. Two reasons could be (1) overemphasis of developmental drilling in old fields, which converted "old" gas to "new" gas under the FPC's definitions, and (2) high profitability of gas sales to the intrastate market at the relatively high new contract prices that prevailed after the Embargo.

The first theory is lent credibility by the fact that, while drilling efforts increased sharply between 1972 and 1976, the number of dry holes did not increase proportionately. This would imply that producers drilling new wells did so in areas where there was a drastically higher probability of finding gas--i.e., in old fields.

Other data supporting the theory that much recent drilling has taken place in and around old fields are those on the

RESERVES IN THE UNITED STATES, 1965-1976 (Mcf)

Total of discoveries, revisions, and extensions	Net change in underground storage	Production*	Proved reserves at end of year	Net change from previous year
21,319,279	150,483	16,252,293	286,468,923	5,217,469
20,220,432	134,523	17,491,073	289,332,805	2,863,882
21,804,333	151,403	18,380,838	292,907,703	3,574,898
13,697,008	118,568	19,373,427	287,349,852	(5,557,851)
8,375,004	107,169	20,723,190	275,108,835	(12,241,017)
37,196,359	402,018	21,960,804	290,746,408	15,637,573
9,825,421	310,301	22,076,512	278,805,618	(11,940,790)
9,634,563	156,563	22,511,898	266,084,846	(12,720,772)
6,825,049	(354,282)	22,605,406	249,950,207	(16,134,639)
8,679,184	(178,424)	21,318,470	237,132,497	(12,817,710)
10,483,688	302,561	19,718,570	228,200,176	(8,932,321)
7,555,468	(187,550)	19,542,020	216,026,074	(12,174,102)

Parentheses denote negative volume.
Source: American Petroleum Institute, Reserves of Crude Oil, Natural Gas Liquids and Natural Gas in the United States and Canada as of December 31, 1976.

sources of reserve additions. As Table 7 indicates, most new reserves come from revisions and extensions of old fields, but this has been more true in recent years, indicating greater concentration of effort in these areas.

Drilling activity on the Outer Continental Shelf (OCS), by definition under the auspices of interstate commerce, showed lackadaisical activity during the 1970s. Table 8 shows the history of OCS drilling activity. Note the decline in total drilling activity and the horizontal trend in gas zone completions.

Allegations of Withholding

There have been numerous allegations involving specific

53

TABLE 8. WELL ACTIVITY--OUTER CONTINENTAL SHELF (1954-1975)

Year	New wells started	Wells completed	Producible zone completions			Dry holes, failures, abandoned
			Oil	Gas	Service	
1954	5	5	3	2	...	2
1955	148	90	59	31	...	15
1956	230	123	98	25	...	87
1957	322	177	133	44	...	109
1958	304	225	174	51	...	126
1959	278	210	162	48	...	72
1960	403	425	333	92	...	106
1961	461	462	337	125	...	114
1962	453	539	409	130	...	135
1963	537	516	421	95	...	216
1964	688	612	507	102	3	241
1965	809	427	538	94	...	290
1966	823	415	528	143	2	464
1967	868	350	455	102	9	359
1968	995	436	550	166	7	346
1969	923	435	520	125	5	446
1970	900	605	681	266	13	357
1971	841	407	393	240	7	449
1972	847	338	306	180	10	448
1973	820	420	304	288	8	506
1974	816	310	226	155	17	547
1975	882	392	225	277	13	546

Source: Department of the Interior, U.S. Geological Survey.

situations where proven reserves of OCS gas purportedly have
been withheld from sale. Withholding of the type alleged
represents a refusal to produce out of existing, known, and
dedicated reserves. This is different from underreporting or
not reporting new reserves, which is often considered withholding as well.

Underreporting or not reporting reserves is the most
difficult charge to substantiate definitively. Substantiation
of the existence of sizeable hidden reserves would require
examination of vast amounts of geological data and the expertise to evaluate it. Moreover, substantial geophysical testing
would be needed to check the data's validity. While the FPC
has attempted to validate the reserve base, its study is the
subject of some controversy.

One of the more important areas of concern is the downward revision of the reserves in old fields. These fields,
many of which are 30 to 40 years old, contain reserves largely
dedicated to the interstate market. Table 9 contains data on
selected fields and producing areas. Dates of discovery show
that most of these fields are old and must have well-known
geology. Although old fields have lower production rates,
large declines in reserves were recorded during short periods
of the past decade. It should be noted that these figures
include reserves added. The downward revisions in pre-existing
reserves, therefore, are substantially understated. With this
in mind, the decline of 2 Tcf in Texas District 3, for example,
appears to be an extraordinary example of "sleight of hand"
with reserve data.

A REALISTIC VIEW OF NATURAL GAS SUPPLY

The rate at which natural gas reserve additions
can become available in the future is critically
dependent on the size of the economically recoverable
undiscovered natural gas resource base. The prevailing
opinion in the past has been that there is a vast
amount of undiscovered natural gas remaining to be
developed in the earth below the lower 48 states and
the adjacent offshore waters. It has also been taken
for granted that this large untapped resource could
be rather readily developed by increasing the mag-
nitude of the industry's exploration incentive by one
means or another. This belief in a vast undiscovered
natural gas resource base has been premised largely
on estimates published over the years by both the
United States Geological Survey (USGS) and by the
Potential Gas Committee (PGC), an industry-sponsored
group. The 1974 USGS estimates of the lower 48
states' undiscovered natural gas resource base range
between 725 and 1,450 trillion cubic feet. The PGC
estimate for undiscovered gas is 568 Tcf.[8]

55

TABLE 9. AMERICAN GAS ASSOCIATION ESTIMATES OF ULTIMATE RECOVERY OF NATURAL GAS, BILLION CUBIC FEET (Bcf), SELECTED YEARS OF RESERVOIR DISCOVERIES AND ESTIMATES

Area	Years			Estimates (Bcf)	
	Discovery	From	Through	From	To
A. Nonassociated					
Texas					
District 1	1953	1970	1974	390.4	206.0
District 2	1963	1967	1970	430.2	187.1
District 3	1935	1970	1973	5,809.5	3,828.3
District 4	1940	1970	1975	1,504.4	854.5
District 7B	1929	1966	1967	74.0	7.4
District 7C	1965	1969	1971	694.1	365.8
District 9	1950	1968	1969	2,442.7	2,204.7
Louisiana					
North	1927	1966	1967	647.1	0.4
South	1959	1969	1973	5,391.4	593.3
B. Associated-Dissolved					
Texas					
District 3	1929	1966	1974	543.7	82.0
District 4	1939	1970	1975	1,714.4	1,147.6
District 5	1933	1969	1970	192.0	142.0
District 6	1930	1967	1974	1,958.1	1,414.5
District 8	1949	1966	1968	1,509.1	76.5
Louisiana					
South	1937	1969	1975	2,939.3	1,925.3

Source: Tabulations prepared by Joseph Lerner from Reserves of Crude Oil, Natural Gas Liquids, and Natural Gas . . . . American Petroleum Institute and American Gas Association, various editions.

The meaningfulness of these large estimates is being increasingly called into question, not only by some of the major oil companies' geologists but by the USGS and the National Academy of Sciences as well. Just one year after issuing the forecasts of potential reserves in the range of 725 to 1,450 Tcf for the lower 48 states (990 to 2,000 Tcf including Alaska), the U.S. Geological Survey (USGS) revised its estimates radically downward. In *Geological Survey Circular 725*, the lower 48 states' reserves were reestimated at 286 to 529 Tcf. The first estimated figure has a 95 percent probability of being fulfilled; the latter only 5 percent. This means that the USGS is 95 percent certain that the 286 Tcf of estimated undiscovered reserves actually exist, but has only a 5 percent level of confidence that 529 Tcf are really in the ground. Figures estimated for Alaska are 29 to 132 Tcf, raising the total estimated U.S. reserve base to the 322 to 655 Tcf range. This is substantially smaller than previous estimates, and it reflects the pessimism with which the nation's reserve base is viewed in the post-Embargo environment. At present production rates, the minimum reserve base in the lower 48 states will only support 14 more years of production at current levels, assuming that all these reserves can indeed be found. Alaskan reserves could probably increase this by 1½ years. With proven nationwide reserves now at about 220 Tcf, including Alaska's 26 Tcf of virtually untapped gas, production possibilities for the remainder of this century do not appear very rosy.

What production levels can realistically be expected from the lower 48 states? The FPC study, *A Realistic View of the U.S. Natural Gas Supply,* provides some interesting insights. Figure 1 shows production capability under various assumptions about reserve additions. The 14.7 Tcf per year figure is the 1960-1975 average for discoveries in the lower 48 states, while 9.5 Tcf per year is the corresponding figure for 1968-1975.

Figure 2 shows the reserve additions needed to support various production growth rates. The 1960-1973 growth rate was 4.3 percent per year, a figure that would require astronomical amounts of new reserves to support.

Estimates of Production Possibilities

Since 1970, numerous forecasts of future production levels have been made, some predicting output in excess of 50 Tcf per year within this century. Table 10 contains a chronological summary of many of them. Looking down the column of forecasts for 1985, the trend over time toward diminishing expected production/consumption levels is clear.

57

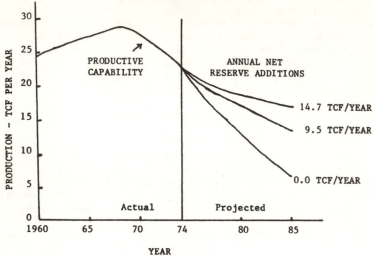

Figure 1

PRODUCTIVE CAPABILITY
LOWER 48 STATES TOTAL SUPPLY

Source: F.P.C., <u>A Realistic View of U.S. Natural Gas Supply</u>

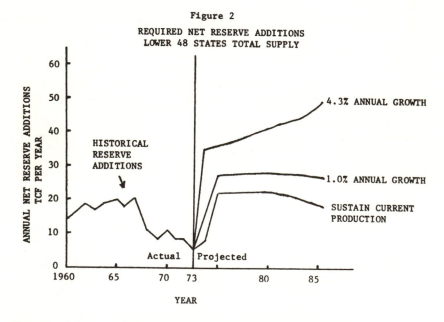

Figure 2

REQUIRED NET RESERVE ADDITIONS
LOWER 48 STATES TOTAL SUPPLY

Source: F.P.C., <u>A Realistic View of U.S. Natural Gas Supply</u>

TABLE 10. FORECASTS OF U.S. NATURAL GAS CONSUMPTION
(trillion of Btu's)

Source	1970	1975	1980	1985	1990	2000
SRI, 1970		23,848	29,871			
WEM, 1970			27,239		35,005	41,693
EBAS, 1970	21,900	26,000	30,400	35,000		
RFF, 1971			27,329		35,005	47,097
BOM, 1971						35,914
NPC, 1971	23,338	22,420	22,480	22,180		57,482
FRC, 1971	26,143[1]	33,906[1]	38,516[1]	43,625[1]	50,115[1]	
RRFF, 1971		23,800	27,500			
PIRF, 1971		26,800	30,600	34,400		
CMB, 1972				27,161		
DOI, 1972		25,220	26,980	28,390		33,980
FPC, 1973		25,009	24,331	25,680	28,870	33,908
FORD, 1974			28,000[2]			32,000[2]
AEC, 1974			29,600[3]			30,500[3]
CEQ, 1974						20,000[4]
LLL, 1974			27,550[5]	29,900[5]		
FEA, 1974			23,140[6]	24,775[6]		
H&J, 1975			26,800	28,022	28,612	28,639
ERDA, 1975			24,000[7]			15,400[7]
FPC, 1975			25,490	26,110	26,006	
CRS, 1975				19,000		
NEO, 1976				22,300		
LEVY, 1976				17,900		
NEO, 1977				16,600		

1. The forecasts are estimates of energy requirements as defined
   by the Future Requirements Committee.
2. Projection offered as scenario possibilities and not predic-
   tions; based on imports cut to half present levels, and
   imports at 3,000,000 barrels per day for 1985-2000.
3. Assumes continuation of past relationship between energy
   consumption and GNP and further increase in the importance of
   electricity as a secondary energy source.
4. Target projection associated with a program of energy conservation and environmental protection.
5. Medium scenario projection.
6. Base-case projection assuming current policies will prevail
   without energy conservation; $11/barrel imported oil.
7. No new initiatives scenario case.

SRI, 1970: Requirements for Southern Louisiana Natural Gas
   through 1980, Federal Power Commission Area Rate Proceedings.
   Exhibit in FPC Docket No. AR69-1, Stanford Research Institute,
   April 1970.

WEM, 1970: "Energy resources and national strength," Auditorium
   Presentation by Warren E. Morrison, Industrial College of the

TABLE 10 (continued)

Armed Forces (transcript and statistical appendix available), Washington, D.C., October 6, 1970.

EBAS, 1970: Energy Consumption and Supply Trends Chart Book. EBASCO Services, Inc., April 1970.

RFF, 1971: Trends and Patterns in U.S. and Worldwide Energy Consumption--A Background Review. Joel Darmstader, Resources for the Future, Inc., Forum on Energy, Economic Growth and the Environment, Washington, D.C., April 20-21, 1971.

BOM, 1971: Mineral Facts and Problems--1970 Edition. Bureau of Mines Bulletin 650, U.S. Department of the Interior, 1971.

NPC, 1971: U.S. Energy Outlook: An Initial Appraisal 1971-1985. Interim Report, National Petroleum Council, 1971.

FRC, 1971: Future Natural Gas Requirements for the United States. Vol. 4, 1971, Future Requirements Committee, Denver Research Institute, University of Denver (under the auspices of the Gas Industry Committee).

RRFF, 1971: "Middle Eastern oil and the Western world: Prospects and problems." Sam H. Schurr and Paul T. Homan, Studies from a Research Program of The Rand Corporation and Resources for the Future, Inc. New York, American Elsevier Publishing Co., 1971.

PIRF, 1971: Oil Import Dependence and Domestic Oil Prices--A 15-Year Forecast in Oil Imports and the National Interest. Henry B. Steele, Petroleum Industry Research Foundation, Inc., March 1971.

CMB, 1972: Outlook for Energy in the United States to 1985. Energy Economics Division, Chase Manhattan Bank, N.A., New York, June 1972.

DOI, 1972: United States Energy through the Year 2000. Walter G. Dupree, Jr., and James A. West, U.S. Department of the Interior, December 1972.

FPC, 1973: Testimony of John N. Nassikas, Chairman, Federal Power Commission, Forecasts by Warren E. Morrison of FPC, Hearings before the Committee on Interior and Insular Affairs, United States Senate, January 11, 1973.

FORD, 1974: A Time to Choose: America's Energy Future. Energy Policy Project, Ford Foundation, 1974.

AEC, 1974: Nuclear Power Growth, 1974-2000. Office of Planning and Analysis, U.S. Atomic Energy Commission, February 1974.

CEQ, 1974: A National Energy Conservation Program: The Half and Half Plan. Russell W. Peterson, Chairman, Council on Environmental Quality, March 1974.

LLL, 1974: An Assessment of U.S. Energy Options for Project Independence. Prepared for the U.S. Atomic Energy Commission under Contract No. W-7405-Eng.-40, Lawrence Livermore Laboratory, University of California, Livermore, September 1974.

FEA, 1974: Project Independence Report, Federal Energy Administration, November 1974.

H&J, 1975: Tax Policy and Energy Conservation, Edward A. Hudson

TABLE 10 (continued)

and Dale W. Jorgenson, Discussion Paper No. 395, Harvard
Institute of Economic Research, January 1975.

ERDA, 1975: A National Plan for Energy Research, Development
and Demonstration: Creating Energy Choices for the Future.
Vol. 1, U.S. Energy Research and Development Administration,
June 1975.

FPC, 1975: "A preliminary evaluation of the cost of natural gas
deregulation," Federal Power Commission, Washington, D.C.

CRS, 1975: Towards Project Interdependence: Energy in the Coming
Decade. Library of Congress, December 1975.

NEO, 1976: National Energy Outlook. Federal Energy Administration, April 1976.

LEVY, 1976: An Assessment of U.S. Energy Policy. September 1976.

NEO, 1977: National Energy Outlook (draft). Federal Energy
Administration, March 1977.

One type of study--the econometric supply analysis--
appears to result in forecasts that are completely out of
line with current thinking about supply levels and prices.
Typical of these efforts is the study by MacAvoy-Pindyck
(1975), whose findings are shown in Table 11. Viewed in 1977,
these forecasts of 1980 production levels at 34.1 Tcf at new
gas prices of $1.00/Mcf dovetail poorly with current per-
ceptions of reality.

Policy Implications of the Reserve Situation

Resource considerations should have a central role in
shaping national gas policy. If the reserve base is indeed
relatively small and if only limited reserve additions can be
anticipated, policies that ration consumption are in order.
On the other hand, if perverse producer behavior under current
and past FPC regulatory practice has led to reserve and
production withholding and if the past ten years of reserve
additions are substantially understated, perhaps current
production levels can be maintained or even enlarged during
the next 25 years.

In fact, large production increases above the present rate
of less than 20 Tcf per year seem unlikely, even under the
more optimistic resource base estimates. The obvious policy
implications are that gas consumption should be discouraged
generally, boiler fuel uses should be terminated, and available
supplies allocated to the highest priority users. There are
two basic approaches (discussed below) to the problem of who
should or should not use gas: (1) administrative end-use
measures and (2) market-determined allocation, using the price
mechanism.

61

TABLE 11. MacAVOY/PINDYCK ECONOMETRIC SIMULATIONS OF PHASED DEREGULATION OF NATURAL GAS

Year	New discoveries (Tcf)	Total additions to reserves (Tcf)	Total reserves (Tcf)	Supply of production (Tcf)	Demands for production (Tcf)	Excess demand for production (Tcf)	New contract field price (¢/Mcf)	Average wholesale price (¢/Mcf)
1972	4.7	8.8	233.4	23.3	23.5	0.2	31.7	39.9
1973	9.9	17.0	227.8	23.6	24.3	0.7	34.7	41.4
1974	10.0	18.4	222.9	24.3	26.3	2.0	39.7	44.3
1975	16.3	24.8	222.3	26.4	28.7	2.3	64.7	52.7
1976	21.4	30.5	226.1	27.6	30.4	2.8	71.7	59.6
1977	25.4	35.3	233.9	28.6	31.9	3.3	78.8	66.3
1978	30.0	41.1	245.8	30.2	32.9	2.7	85.9	73.7
1979	31.5	43.9	258.6	32.1	33.7	1.6	93.1	81.1
1980	33.0	45.6	271.2	34.1	34.2	0.1	100.3	88.3

Source: American Enterprise Institute, Price Controls and The Natural Gas Shortage, Table 8.

PRODUCTION ECONOMICS AND RISING PRICES

One important effect of the large rise in oil and gas
prices has been a correspondingly large increase in apparent
production costs. Key cost elements tend to track prices.
This clearly occurred in 1974 and 1975 as producers bid eagerly
for limited inputs of land, labor, and equipment, raising the
"rents" to these inputs, which in turn absorbed portions of
the would-be profits. Certain factors of production have
flexible values that will adjust upward or downward, roughly
paralleling energy price levels. Among these are the mineral
rights to geologically attractive, potential gas-producing
areas, which are limited in supply. Mineral rights to federal
lands are usually auctioned to producers on the basis of a
lump-sum bid. A limited supply of leases, coupled with high
gas prices or expectations thereof, results in the capture of
some of the economic rents from this gas by the U.S. Treasury.
In the past, lease offerings have been limited in order to
maximize the Treasury's revenue. How the government's interest
in maximizing leasing revenues dovetails with resource development goals is a matter that deserves much further consideration.

Royalties and other financial considerations paid to
private and state landowners also have shown upward flexibility
in response to higher post-Embargo oil and gas prices.
Royalties have tended to increase from one-sixteenth to one-
eighth share of wellhead selling prices, and royalty interests
have captured an increasing share of price increases. Through
royalty payments, rents are redistributed to owners of mineral-
bearing lands.

Equipment prices are not as flexible as those of mineral
rights although they do retain some flexibility, especially
rates for rented equipment. As gas prices and drilling activity
rose within the past four years, prices of both oil field
materials and rig rentals rose sharply. Apparently, the producers and owners of drilling rigs and materials collected
some of the quasi-rents that would otherwise have been earned
by oil and gas producers. If this experience is a guide, it
seems clear that some portion of future gas price increases
would be redistributed to the oil field material supply sector.
If gas prices are constrained at lower levels, some of these
scarcity payments will be avoided.

A specialized labor pool is also required to supply the
unique skills necessary for oil and gas exploration. Once
again, the upsurge in oil field activity occurred in the face
of a relatively inelastic supply of these skills. The result
was a rapid boost in the wages and salaries of workers with
oil field skills. This component of costs tends to be ratcheted
into place; especially through bidding-up labor costs, the
upsurge in oil and gas prices has created a higher cost industry
than would have existed with less sudden and more orderly price
increases.

This has two implications. First, higher prices beget higher production costs rather than resulting from cost increases. Second, if prices are constrained, a primary effect will be on the levels of certain rents and quasi-rents, which will have minimal effects on supply availability and drilling activity.

The Decision To Produce Known Reserves

A producer owning proven reserves or property where gas is likely to be found faces a decision of whether to sell at current prices or to postpone production until prices rise. The decision will be based largely on the rate of return that can be earned by holding gas compared with that of alternative investments into which the gas sale revenues can be invested. A producer could, in theory, market gas at current prices and invest the proceeds in a financial asset that provides some rate of return. Alternatively, he can hold gas in the ground in the hope that prices will rise. If the rate of price increase is higher than the return on alternative investments, a producer will be better off holding gas. In this situation, gas in the ground can be a better investment than money in the bank.

A simple but relevant example of how this works can be presented. Consider a producer who could produce and deliver gas in 1970 but chose not to do so. Let us assume that the rate for that gas was then 20¢/Mcf, a typical new gas price for that year. If the producer delayed selling those reserves until 1976, when the national rate of $1.42 became effective, his 20¢ gas has increased in value by 470 percent. Had the producer sold the gas in 1970, he would have had to find an investment that yielded 38.5 percent annually to equal the return on investment attributable to gas left in the ground.

A strong incentive existed here to withhold gas, and the incentive continues to be strong as long as prices are expected to increase at annual rates that are higher than the return on other readily available investments. Anticipation of deregulation or rapid biennial increases in the national rate encourage such behavior. These two factors have created an environment that fosters production holdbacks. They function because there has been no clear-cut policy, articulated without ambivalence, stating that natural gas price increases will be limited to moderate amounts. Such a clear-cut policy statement will greatly diminish the withholding incentive. This policy can provide for annual price escalators so long as these maintain the return on holding gas in the ground equal to or lower than the rate of return on alternative investments. And this should certainly be a goal of natural gas regulatory legislation.

At prices equal to or less than oil fuel equivalents, the potential demand for gas is extremely large and can be estimated roughly by the shortfall in domestic energy production, which in turn is measured by oil imports. Since the early 1970s, gas production has been the factor limiting consumption, and supply constraints will continue indefinitely to limit perceived demand under most resource projections.

About 28 percent of current domestic energy consumption is imported, the equivalent of about 17 Tcf of natural gas. This shortfall is nearly equal to current gas output. If this amount of output could be achieved at prices lower than or equal to the equivalent of imported oil, imports would be displaced entirely.

Demand Elasticity

Estimating the demand elasticity for gas is a complex problem that is nevertheless central to a determination of the efficacy of price as a conservation tool. Numerous attempts have been made over the years to estimate both short- and long-term price effects. Lester Taylor has compiled a useful historical summary of thought in this area.[10] For the most part, these estimates suggest relatively high elasticities (i.e., greater than 1) for the long run. This implies that price would be a relatively effective conservation tool, although some time would be required before the full effects would be realized. In general, Taylor's summary of econometric estimates, shown in Table 12, indicates that conservation might be achieved effectively through the price mechanism.

The most current and extensive work on demand elasticity is being done by the Federal Energy Administration (FEA). On the basis of a dynamic model that focuses on year-to-year shifts, FEA economists are able to trace the transition in consumption patterns as gas prices rise relatively slowly toward equivalency with oil. Changes in the stock of gas-burning equipment, which are a function of time, are accounted for, as are the inter-fuel substitutions facilitated by equipment changes. The dynamics of the model are important because they take account of the fact that reaction times of gas users are at least partly a function of the procurement cycle for new equipment using different fuels or for energy-saving devices and more efficient facilities. Table 13 presents the FEA estimates.

The main drawback of price-induced conservation is that, according to most estimates, it is relatively ineffective in the short run. As time progresses and users can switch to other fuels or carry out conservation efforts, price effects on demand become more pronounced. The drawback stems from

TABLE 12. PRICE ELASTICITIES OF NATURAL GAS DEMAND:
SUMMARY OF ECONOMETRIC ESTIMATES

Type of demand	Price elasticity	
	Short-run	Long-run
Residential		
Verhulst (1950)	..	-3.00
Felton (1965)	..	-1.72
Houthakker and Taylor (1970)	0	0
Anderson (1973)	..	-1.73
Randall, Ives, and Ryan (1974)	..	-1.12
FEA (1976)	-0.16	-1.26
Commercial		
Felton (1965)	..	-1.45
FEA (1976)	-0.38	large
Residential-Commercial		
Balestra (1967)	small	-0.70
Berndt and Watkins (1975)	-0.20	-0.90
Industrial		
Vermetten and Plantinga (1953)	..	-2.11
Felton (1965)	..	-1.50
Anderson (1971)	..	-1.98
MacAvoy and Noll (1973)	..	-1.78
FEA (1976)	-0.17	-0.58
Commercial-Industrial		
Randall, Ives, and Ryan (1974)	..	-3.85
Total Retail Sales	..	-1.91

The data in this table are taken from unpublished observations
by various workers in the field, cited in Lester Taylor, 1976,
"The Demand for Energy, a Survey of Price and Income
Elasticities."

the fact that conservation must be paid for, in terms of high
prices, in early years when there are few savings as well as
in later years when benefits are a more substantial offset to
costs.

There seems to be a fundamental conflict between the 1977
FEA estimates in Table 13 and the earlier studies summarized
by Taylor, inasmuch as the FEA estimates very low long-run
elasticities (less than -1.0) and especially low elasticities
for the industrial buyer. This can be explained by recognizing that, at burner-tip prices equal to or below those of
oil fuels, gas savings come only from conservation through more
efficient use, installation of energy-saving devices, and other
such measures, not from fuel switching.

TABLE 13.   PRICE ELASTICITIES OF NATURAL GAS DEMAND BY
CONSUMING SECTOR, 1977-1985

Year	Commercial	Residential	Industrial	Total
1977	−0.403	−0.332	−0.213	−0.268
1978	−0.490	−0.388	−0.264	−0.331
1979	−0.559	−0.428	−0.297	−0.358
1980	−0.614	−0.458	−0.318	−0.382
1981	−0.659	−0.481	−0.333	−0.399
1982	−0.696	−0.499	−0.343	−0.411
1983	−0.726	−0.514	−0.350	−0.420
1984	−0.751	−0.526	−0.356	−0.426
1985	−0.773	−0.535	−0.360	−0.431

Source: Federal Energy Administration.

Conservation through Regulation

A certain amount of conservation occurs through the curtailment plan now being used by the FPC. This plan, which really was designed for small, transitory supply shortfalls, curtails large-volume users first and moves to smaller users as shortfalls become more serious. Its underlying logic is that larger users can switch to other fuels more easily than smaller consumers during shortage periods. In Order 467B, the FPC has established a schedule of priorities based on volume of usage rather than on ability to use alternative fuels. "Quality" of use is ignored here also, because essential users with no ready gas substitutes usually are curtailed as much as boiler fuel users. Over time, curtailments will move down the priority list to smaller users, and supply interruptions will affect more users for longer periods.

The FPC's curtailment plan should be updated to recognize the chronic nature of the shortage. Priorities should be ordered to indicate clearly who should receive gas and how much each recipient should get. Boiler fuel users and other low "quality" consumption could be eliminated and essential uses protected from shortfalls to the extent possible. However, property rights are established, and some arbitrary and perhaps capricious decisions must be made. Milton Russell summarizes well the problem involved:

The value of this right to gas is substantial.
Its distribution to the selected consumers is

fortuitous or discriminatory. This points up
important issues that will continue to bedevil
gas regulators: What are appropriate criteria
for priority access to gas, and what are the
proper quantity of special relief to be granted
and the proper criteria for granting it? To the
extent that some gas is allocated to the "de-
serving," another group of the dispossessed
is created. In property distribution terms,
whether this distribution will be perceived
as equitable or not is an open question. One
thing is certain: continuation of the current
policy, or one similar to it, grants to the
FPC enormous economic power in allowing or per-
mitting some firms or individuals to obtain a
fuel supply substantially below its opportunity
cost.[11]

Russell expresses further concern about the effects of
mandatory allocation on income distribution. With the creation
of property rights, income in the form of fuel priced below
other energy users' cost accrues to those having access to
price-controlled gas. Envision two competing firms, one
manufacturing a product using an allocation of price-controlled
gas and the other, less fortunate company burning oil. The
firm allocated gas clearly has a production cost advantage
vis-a-vis its oil-using competitor, and this will show up in
higher profits for the firm with the gas allocation. In effect,
income has been transferred between these firms or between
any other individuals similarly situated in the gas allocation
scheme. Russell suggests that gas property rights be made
marketable, so that optional allocation might be moved as gas:
entitlement holders could auction off their rights. In this
way, gas users who wanted to or could switch to other fuels
or who could conserve would be rewarded by the profits from
selling their gas allocations. Those needing gas enough to
pay the higher price could obtain it.

Something of this nature occurred during the 1976-1977
winter emergency. Facilitated by the Emergency Natural Gas Act
of 1977, the FPC approved a temporary sale of intrastate gas
that previously had been used by an electric utility at
$3.05/Mcf. This price was designed to reimburse the utility
for its cost of using residual fuel plus storage costs and
compensation for generation efficiency lost. This type of
transaction illustrates the feasibility of regulatory measures
aimed at improving allocation. Regulatory procedures encouraging transactions of this type on an even broader basis
should be explored further or perhaps legislatively mandated
on at least an experimental basis.

Other Curtailment-related Problems

The FPC implements curtailments of interstate pipeline sales to local gas distribution systems. For the most part, curtailments to actual end users are allocated by these local distributors. The FPC's curtailment priorities do not necessarily determine the pattern of rationing by local utilities.

Another problem not addressed by present curtailment policy is the regional maldistribution of the shortages: certain parts of the country are curtailed more seriously than others because they are served by pipelines that were less fortunate or less energetic in lining up gas reserves during the 1950s and 1960s when supplies were more readily available. While this problem was addressed on a temporary and limited basis by the Emergency Natural Gas Act of 1977, there is a need to turn curtailments--as long as they are necessary--into a meaningful allocation tool. A legislative remedy appears in order, facilitating some form of mandatory allocation among pipelines.

Nationwide industrial conservation on an even-handed basis can be achieved if all pipelines curtail the same categories of industrial consumption to the same degree. With the current curtailment situation, some pipelines' industrial customers, including large boiler fuel users, are served virtually without interruption. Industrial customers of other pipelines have been deeply curtailed, even those users requiring gas for essential uses where fuel substitution is an extremely costly matter.

Allocation of supplies among pipelines such that industrial curtailment ends most boiler fuel and other low value uses is desirable. As a matter of national policy, uniform end-use controls--which essentially means phasing out large boiler fuel users--can be implemented, while at the same time curtailments can be managed on a nationwide basis. Regional equity can be achieved as well, ending the imbalances that stem from some regions' pipelines being better supplied than others.

Conservation through means other than price can be achieved in the residential sector. The Carter Administration's program of tax credits for installing insulation and other energy-saving equipment addresses this as well as or perhaps better than the price approach. If demand elasticities are as low as estimated by FEA, conservation by means other than higher prices could well be more cost-effective, particularly during the first five to ten years.

ECONOMIC IMPACTS FROM GAS PRICE INCREASES

During 1974 and 1975, the nation experienced sharp increases in the price of crude oil and oil products, unregulated

intrastate natural gas, and coal. All told, these fuels'
prices had increased $54 billion by the end of 1975. The
rapid escalation of energy prices had a profound macroeconomic
impact.

During this period of rising energy prices, the GNP
deflator rose by 19.2 percent, the GNP itself declined 1.9
percent, and unemployment rose from 4.8 percent to 8.3 percent
at the end of 1975 (down from 8.9 percent in May 1975). Thus,
energy price increases accounted directly for one quarter of
the 1974-1975 inflation, inasmuch as the $54 billion energy
price increase added more than four percentage points to the
nominal GNP. The total effects, compounded by the draconian
monetary policy of that period, accounted for perhaps one-half
of the decline in GNP during these two years.

While the need for higher gas prices is seen by many,
the alternative of deregulation carries with it implications
of macroeconomic energy shock that goes far beyond simply
providing higher producer prices. A rapid run-up of gas
prices will set in motion powerful inflationary forces. Most
legislative proposals attempt to mitigate this in one way or
another, but the potential price increases involved are substantial.

Estimating Potential Deregulation Costs

There have been numerous proposals for deregulation or
changes in the guidelines for regulation of new natural gas
prices. Concern has been expressed about the overall cost of
deregulation, as well as the effect of rapid price increases
on the economy.

The key variables in computing deregulation impacts are:
1. the new gas definition, which determines the volume
    of gas subject to price increases
2. the ceiling or market clearing level to which
    prices would rise
3. whether intrastate gas is included under the
    ceiling if one is imposed
4. how old, flowing gas is treated, and what pro-
    visions are made to enforce delivery of old gas
    previously contracted for.

Outright Deregulation: A Worst Case Scenario

For an illustration, we will assume that a law is enacted
that relieves the FPC of all responsibilities to regulate
wellhead prices. Under this worst case scenario, forces are
set in motion that cause both interstate and intrastate gas
prices to rise quickly to $3.00/Mcf, something which most
deregulation bills ostensibly seek to avoid.

I believe that the $3.00/Mcf is a conservative price
assumption, at least for the near term. Even under incremental

70

pricing (discussed below), interstate pipelines, which have
suffered large curtailments, will compete vigorously for whatever new gas or available old intrastate supplies are forth-
coming. In doing this, the interstate pipelines will have the
advantage of being able to bid high prices and roll the expensive incremental gas in with still controlled old gas and still
deliver a product for a blended price at or lower than competitive fuels. In 1978 or 1979, when any deregulation legislation
passed might take effect, the competitive fuel will be middle
distillate. This light oil fuel is expected to sell for
nearly 50¢/gallon by the end of 1978 under the crude oil
equalization tax and other crude oil and refiner cost increases. This is the equivalent of $3.60/Mcf delivered gas.
Subtracting out delivery charges applicable to industrial users
of about 75¢/Mcf, we would have a Btu-equivalent wellhead
price of just under $3.00/Mcf. However, pipelines may well
pay prices substantially in excess of $3.00--perhaps as high
as $5.00--during deregulation's first and possibly second
years because of their ability to roll in new with old gas.
This tendency will be further reinforced by some customers'
willingness to pay prices above oil equivalent rather than bear
the expense of converting to an alternative fuel.

Intrastate Gas

     Interstate pipelines, hard-pressed for new supplies, would
bid for gas heretofore confined to intrastate markets. Given
limited supplies and the relative flexibility of intrastate
gas contracts, prices rise quickly. New and renegotiated intrastate prices averaged about $1.85/Mcf in 1977. Without con-
straints on interstate prices, virtually all intrastate supplies
easily could rise to about $3.00 within a short period as the
pipeline buyers compete in a seller's market. With present
consumption at 8 Tcf, the total cost to intrastate consumers
would be $9.2 billion [($3 - $1.85/Mcf) X 8 billion Mcf]. The
full impact of this increase could occur within perhaps two
years, as existing intrastate contracts are broken and renegotiated and as prices are escalated under a variety of
provisions facilitating such adjustments.
     Intrastate gas consumers have long been unintended bene-
ficiaries of federal interstate regulation. Meanwhile, they
have enjoyed ample gas supplies. Thus, these users would be
among the earliest and largest losers from a policy of deregulation, as interstate pipelines aggressively enter markets
formerly reserved for intrastate demand. Consumers in these
markets previously protected from outside demand would be among
the first to appreciate how an unregulated market for natural
gas operates.

"Rolled-over" gas

     Under present FPC practice, as older contracts between

71

TABLE 14. ROLL-OVER OF OLD INTERSTATE AND FLOWING VOLUMES
(Bcf)

Year	First rolled-over in current year	Cumulative flowing gas
1974	381	—
1975	175	529
1976	120	612
1977	285	854
1978	282	1,077
1979	347	1,348
1980	383	1,637
1981	261	1,783

Source: Estimated from Appendix A of FPC Opinion 699H using a 6 percent decline rate.

producers and interstate pipelines expire, this gas continues to flow in interstate commerce at 52¢/Mcf. With deregulation, this practice would be terminated and prices would rise to a scarcity price of $3.00.

Table 14 contains a tabulation of the gas volumes involved through 1981. Costs in terms of higher prices are calculated in Table 15 for the amounts of gas that would rise to unregulated prices under this scenario. Rolled-over gas would rise--like other gas--to $3.00/Mcf. This reflects the assumption that this old gas otherwise would be produced at 52¢ and that the additional $2.48/Mcf would add nothing to the volume of production in this category.

New Gas

As production from old wells in known fields declines, new wells are drilled, tapping both known and new reserves. About 80 percent of the new reserves are from extensions of old fields through additional development drilling. Table 7 showed both the limited amount of new field discoveries and the relatively large reserve additions from extensions and revisions of existing fields. Gas discovered as an extension of old fields is different from new field discoveries in that new field discoveries are the result of much riskier wildcatting. Nevertheless, under present regulations and also

72

TABLE 15.   DEREGULATION COST SUMMARY

Cost element	1978		1979	
	Vol (Tcf)	$ (bil)	Vol (Tcf)	$ (bil)
Intrastate gas	4.0	4.6	8.0	9.2
Rolled-over gas	1.1	2.7	1.3	3.4
Renegotiated contracts	3.8	9.5	3.8	9.5
New gas	1.0	1.5	2.0	3.0
Redrilling of old fields for definitionally new gas	1.0	2.5	2.0	5.0
Total	10.9	20.8	17.1	30.1

Source: Author's calculations.

with decontrol, no distinction is made between new gas that is
hard to find (i.e., new gas from new fields) and that which
is much less risky and expensive (i.e., "new" gas from old
fields).

It is in part for this reason that some new gas has been
dedicated to the interstate market even under FPC regulation.
We estimate that 1 Tcf per year of new gas production would be
available to the interstate market under Opinion 770 rates
($1.42 plus adjustments). Given the limitations of resource
base discussed above, little additional gas can be expected to
appear in response to price increases above these levels in
real dollar rates. Thus, we can consider the escalating new
gas price as a pure scarcity cost. This may be computed as
$1.5 billion annually [1 billion Mcf X ($3.00 - $1.45)].

Renegotiated Contracts

A recent study by the General Accounting Office (GAO)
estimated that many pipeline/producer contracts have a variety
of pricing clauses that facilitate price escalation in the
event of deregulation.[12] The amounts of gas for which prices
might be adjusted could be limited by statute or by FPC
administrative measures. The GAO report describes several
generic types of clauses:
- renegotiation clauses that allow for price changes
  in response to some specific events
- redetermination clauses that are similar to
  renegotiation clauses in their effect and provide
  for price escalations to the "fair market price"

73

or some negotiated price that may be higher than
the pre-existing FPC ceiling

- "most favored nation" clauses that allow for increased rates if prices in other contracts in the
  field rise
- deregulation clauses that permit higher rates in
  the event regulatory control is removed
- area-rate clauses that allow prices to escalate
  to the highest rate established by FPC for the
  area covered by the contract.

GAO also notes that only the area-rate clause appears to
be permissible under FPC administrative regulations. Furthermore, the GAO reports that

- 26 percent of the interstate gas supplies is sold
  under contract having renegotiation or redetermination clauses
- 10 percent is under contract with favored nation
  clauses
- 2 percent is under contracts having deregulation
  clauses.

Thus, more than one-third of all interstate gas supplies are
affected by these clauses. Some contracts, however, have more
than one escalator provision. It is estimated that some 3.8
Tcf of existing interstate gas supplies would escalate in
price during the first year of deregulation unless the deregulation statute specifically prohibited this. With this
gas today averaging less than 50¢/Mcf, an increase of $2.50/Mcf
would cost gas users $9.5 billion annually (3.8 billion Mcf
X $2.50). Costs would build up to this level by about the end
of the first year of deregulation.

Redrilling of Old Fields

"New" natural gas is currently defined by the FPC as gas
from a new well, spudded on or after a specified date. In
Opinion 770A, this was modified to exclude recompletions of
existing wells to tap shallower gas-bearing strata through
which the well already passes but from which the well does not
produce. As the price differential between old and new gas
widens, incentives to drilling new wells to tap "old" reserves
become greater. This is clearly the easiest way to obtain new
gas, and with the trebling of regulated new gas prices between
1974 and 1976, some of this type of activity must be occurring.
Statistics on drilling and reserve addition lend credence to
this theory.

A large number of gas wells have been drilled and
completed in recent years with disproportionately small reserve
additions. One can infer, among other reasons for the
apparently low productivity of drilling, that some of these
wells were drilled to obtain "new" gas from old reserves.
Under deregulation legislation, which does not address this

74

tactic directly, we believe that 1 Tcf per year of gas will
be liberated from its current price ceilings in this fashion.
It will rise from an estimated average of 50¢/Mcf to $3.00, a
$2.50 increase.

Table 15 summarizes the total effect of the various factors
that will act together to raise costs. Under unqualified
deregulation, gas users would be paying an estimated $35
billion in higher prices by 1980 if deregulation occurred in
late 1977.

The impact of price increases of this size on the economy
can only add to inflation, while disrupting and reducing employ-
ment and production. Although smaller in total cost than the
1974-1975 energy price rise and affecting an economy that is
perhaps 25 or 30 percent larger in current dollars, these price
increases would raise price indices by as much as one and a
half percentage points in 1978 and by a slightly smaller amount
in 1979.

MINIMIZING THE IMPACT OF DEREGULATION

There really is no truly free competitive market for oil
and gas in the world today. Either the U.S. government sets
certain maximum gas prices, or it pays minimum gas prices set
indirectly by OPEC. The choice is whether the American producer should be permitted to ride on OPEC's coattails while
U.S. consumers pay cartel prices for gas from their own
national patrimony (even from federal lands), or whether one
or both will face a lower price administered by the U.S.
government. Because of the recent large price rises and the
limited response of supply to higher prices, the payoff to
still higher prices is questionable.

A number of ceiling price concepts are frequently discussed that would result in higher wellhead prices but would
avoid the uncontrolled escalation that would occur with deregulation. In general, these limits are most often associated
with Btu equivalency with oil fuels of some type. A nationwide
ceiling price based on an oil equivalency would do two things.
First, it would prevent prices from escalating to undesirably
high levels, perhaps even higher than Btu equivalency with
light oil fuels (well over $3.00/Mcf) for some transitory
period. Second, intrastate and interstate prices could be
equilibrated at a below-market clearing level in a scarcity
environment. The demise of the two-tiered price would certainly mitigate nationwide allocation.

Defining New Gas

The most important variable in computing the cost of
various proposals to raise gas prices is the language that
determines how much gas will qualify for the higher rates. If
little gas is eligible, the aggregate impact can be small,

75

even with a very high new gas price. Conversely, if relatively large amounts of gas are allowed to rise in price over
a short period, consumer costs can be great.

There are great differences of opinion as to what should
and should not qualify as new gas. Output that is considered
new by a producer is considered to be old gas by many who would
have to pay the bill. Figure 3 shows six general classes of
drilling activity. For many industry partisans, new gas is
that from any new well in any formation, because drilling any
well involves expenditure of new capital. For others, new
gas is that from a new pool, even if that pool is in an old,
already known field. Similarly, an extension of an existing
pool might be considered to yield new gas. The most strict
definition of new gas, however, is that from a new pool in a
new field. This is the most important type of discovery and,
during recent years, the most rare. Table 7 indicates that
only a small fraction of annual reserve additions have come
from development drilling or extensions of old fields as well as
from new pools found in old fields.

Narrowing the new gas definition to exclude reserves added
via extension and development drilling reduces the amount of
new gas by perhaps 60 percent from what it would be if all
reserve additions qualified. This helps to focus drilling
activity on finding new pools. It also reserves high wellhead
prices for gas for which the risk and thus the cost is greatest.
Moreover, from the standpoint of curbing the burden of higher
gas prices on consumers and the economy, such limitations have
the effect of making smaller amounts of gas eligible for higher
prices.

While the limitation of higher prices to new pool discoveries helps to focus drilling efforts on truly new gas, a
definition aimed at encouraging exploration for and development
of completely new, geographically distinct fields addresses
the supply problem even more incisively. This would place
the incentive on exploration outside traditional producing
areas and encourage producers to look for new fields rather
than expend their efforts on developing and extending largely
depleted old fields.

On the other hand, lower prices for gas in and around
old fields should not be detrimental to supply, because full
exploitation of already known producing areas should be
profitable at prices greatly below the new field incentive
price.

The New Oil Definition

In distinguishing new from old crude oil, the FEA has
adopted a definition based on property lines. Under this
definition, production from new property (where there has
never before been production) is rewarded with an incentive
price. Such a concept creates incentives to lease mineral

76

Figure 3 - CLASSIFICATION OF GAS WELLS

OBJECTIVE OF DRILLING	INITIAL CLASSIFICATION WHEN DRILLING IS STARTED	FINAL CLASSIFICATION AFTER COMPLETION OR ABANDONMENT	
		SUCCESSFUL	UNSUCCESSFUL
Drilling for a new field on a structure or in an environment never before productive	1. NEW-FIELD WILDCAT	NEW-FIELD DISCOVERY WILDCAT	DRY NEW-FIELD WILDCAT
Drilling for a new pool on a structure or in a geological environment already productive — Drilling outside limits of a proved area of pool	2. NEW-POOL (PAY) WILDCAT	NEW-POOL DISCOVERY WILDCAT (NEW-POOL DISCOVERY WELLS)	DRY NEW-POOL WILDCAT (DRY NEW-POOL TESTS)
NEW POOL TESTS — Drilling inside limits of proved area of pool — For a new pool below deepest proven pool	3. DEEPER POOL (PAY) TEST	DEEPER POOL DISCOVERY WELL (NEW-POOL DISCOVERY WELLS)	DRY DEEPER POOL TEST (DRY NEW-POOL TESTS)
For a new pool above deepest proven pool	4. SHALLOWER POOL (PAY) TEST	SHALLOWER POOL DISCOVERY WELL (NEW-POOL DISCOVERY WELLS)	DRY SHALLOWER POOL TEST
Drilling for long extension of a partly developed pool	5. OUTPOST or EXTENSION TEST	EXTENSION WELL	DRY OUTPOST OR DRY EXTENSION TEST
Drilling to exploit or develop a hydrocarbon accumulation discovered by previous drilling	6. DEVELOPMENT WELL	DEVELOPMENT WELL	DRY DEVELOPMENT WELL

Source: Fred J. Wagner and Charles F. Higlehart, "North American drilling activity in 1973," American Association of Petroleum Geologists Bulletin, vol. 58, p. 1501.

rights and explore in previously unexplored locations, thus fostering the search for truly new resources.

Price Adjustments under Existing Contracts

The GAO study cited above indicates that the potential scope of gas price increases is considerably expanded by the fact that gas producers have long anticipated sharply higher prices and have written both interstate and intrastate contracts with this in mind. Most intrastate gas and about one-third of the interstate gas flows under contracts with adjustable pricing provisions that permit escalation of old gas prices as those for new gas go up. These clauses would permit escalations in the prices of much already flowing gas to occur within a year or two after new prices rise.

The Emergency Natural Gas Act of 1977 attempted to prevent this. The law, which expired after the winter of 1977, prohibited activation of escalation or termination clauses that otherwise would be brought into force by the higher prices paid under this legislation during the emergency sales that it facilitated.

Because an estimated 12 Tcf per year are sold under interstate and intrastate contracts containing flexible pricing clauses, inclusion of statements specifically prohibiting the operation of escalation clauses in any bill raising new gas prices is an important step in holding down old gas prices. Such statements would be especially important to protect intrastate markets.

Incremental Pricing

A proposal often discussed for limiting the effects of higher prices on homeowners is so-called incremental pricing. Under this plan, the higher costs of new gas are allocated to industrial users only. Proponents of this scheme claim that it has four benefits:

1. It protects residential users from price rises for some time.
2. It tends to prevent pipelines from paying prices above the oil equivalent after some period.
3. Intrastate consumers are protected from prices significantly above the oil equivalent, because interstate pipelines will not drive intrastate prices markedly above these levels.
4. A market test for new gas is provided.

In reality, these contentions are not as clear-cut as incremental pricing's supporters might hold. As pipelines deplete low-cost old gas and replace these supplies with expensive new gas, higher costs are allocated to the pipeline systems' industrial customers. Gas utilities sell about 7 Tcf per year to industrial users, and some of this current old gas will be replaced in the normal course of events by new gas. Competition among pipelines, if unrestrained, could escalate the price of scarce new gas supplies to as high as $5.00/Mcf or perhaps to even higher levels.

Let us assume that pipeline systems add 3 Tcf per year of new gas over a two- or three-year period at the $5.00/Mcf price. This will be blended in with 4 Tcf per year of flowing old gas at 50¢/Mcf. We can compute the blended price as:

$$
\begin{array}{rcl}
4 \text{ Tcf} \times \$0.50/\text{Mcf} & = & \$2 \text{ billion} \\
3 \text{ Tcf} \times \$5.00/\text{Mcf} & = & \underline{\$15 \text{ billion}} \\
& & \$17 \text{ billion}
\end{array}
$$

With the pipeline systems' total gas bill at $17 billion during that year, the average Mcf will cost $2.40 plus transport. Nonetheless, pipelines will have paid prices much higher than oil equivalency for the new supplies and passed these costs along to end users without any one end user paying the true incremental price. Thus, incremental pricing would not necessarily impose restraint on gas pipelines' bidding for supplies in the initial years of the new regulations.

During the transitional period when pipelines are able in this fashion to bid up new gas prices to levels well above oil-equivalent prices, intrastate prices will rise sharply unless somehow constrained. Interstate pipelines, which can pay these exceptionally high prices and still compete for customers, will attempt to bid old as well as new gas away from intrastate markets. Because they will be able to pay higher prices, intrastate prices will be subject to terrific strains, and they will rise above the oil-equivalent levels. With few constraints on old interstate prices, instate consumers will see surprisingly large price increases.

Protecting Intrastate Gas Consumers

As intrastate prices have risen, calls for some sort of protection have come from consumers in most of the producing states. The New Mexico legislature, in fact, has imposed a ceiling on instate gas prices, setting it at the FPC's latest national rates. Recent proposals before Congress seem to recognize the need to protect consumers of intrastate gas, either by applying a nationwide ceiling both to intrastate and interstate markets or by freezing old intrastate gas prices in one manner or another.

The application of uniform nationwide ceilings would appear to offer the same protection from runaway prices to all consumers. This would also circumvent some of the mis-allocation of supplies that arises from buyers in an uncon-trolled submarket bidding gas away from a controlled submarket. Given the apparent limitations of the gas resource base, this seems to make sense.

Another proposal would protect intrastate users by imposing a ceiling on old intrastate gas prices. This would prevent interstate pipelines from escalating the price of this gas. It would protect intrastate consumers to the extent that old intrastate gas remained "old" under the deregulating legislation's new gas definition.

EQUITY CONSIDERATIONS--A CONCLUDING NOTE

As natural gas prices rise from their present average of 60¢/Mcf, it is clear that producer revenues will increase. If prices rise to oil-equivalent levels or higher, gross revenues of gas producers will rise markedly, especially those of the 25 largest firms who produce 80 percent of the nation's gas. To the extent that these revenues become profits and are not consumed by higher costs, wealth will be redistributed from consumers to producers. Consumers who buy goods and services will ultimately bear the burden of higher gas prices, as the industrial and commercial sectors pass along these fuel costs.

Even if there are no windfall profits from higher gas prices, monies will be redistributed to the supply sectors that provide the factors of production used for gas exploration and development. Since these firms and individuals are located largely in the Southwest, regional income redistribution can be expected as monies from consuming (and nonproducing) states flow to firms and individuals located in the Southwestern producing areas. Funds will be geographically redistributed from the "snowbelt" states to the "sunbelt" states.

NOTES

1. 15 U.S. Code 717.

2. 347 U.S. Code 672, *Phillips Petroleum Co.* v. *Wisconsin*, 1954.

3. Clark A. Hawkins, *The Field Price Regulation of Natural Gas* (Tallahassee: Florida State University Press, 1969), p. 23.

4. Robert B. Helms, *Natural Gas Regulation: An Evaluation of FPC Price Control* (Washington, D.C.: American Enterprise Institute for Public Policy Research, 1974), p. 19.

5. Hawkins, op. cit., p. 77-78.

6. One thousand cubic feet (1 Mcf) of gas contains an average of about 1,030,000 Btus.

7. Opinion 770 rates are being collected subject to refund due to the fact that this decision is the subject of several legal suits.

8. "A realistic view of U.S. natural gas supply." FPC Staff Report, December 1974.

9. Paul MacAvoy and Robert S. Pindyck, *Price Controls and the Natural Gas Shortage* (Washington, D.C.: American Enterprise Institute for Public Policy Research, 1975).

10. Lester Taylor, *The Demand for Energy: A Survey of Price and Income Elasticities*, 1976, Table 4.

11. Milton Russell, "Natural gas curtailments: Administrative rationing or market allocation?," in Harry Trebing, ed., *New Dimensions in Public Utility Pricing* (East Lansing: Michigan State University, 1976).

12. "Selected contract sales: Information related to the deregulation of natural gas." GAO Report, 1975.

4

Applying Marginal Cost Analysis to the Rate Structure for Natural Gas Sales to Ultimate Customers

Philip J. Mause

INTRODUCTION

Discussions concerning the natural gas issue are usually dominated by the debate concerning the regulation or deregulation of wellhead gas. That debate has become more complicated, and the relevant issue more and more appears to be "What is the right regulated price for new natural gas?" A much less publicized issue has been the question of the rate structures under which transmission and distribution utilities sell natural gas to ultimate consumers.

In the course of the regulation-deregulation debate, arguments concerning the importance of presenting a correct "price signal" to consumers in order to encourage efficient use of natural gas have frequently been raised. These price signals, the actual rates that confront the end users of natural gas, are an important and often neglected issue in the public policy debate concerning natural gas. After all, it is the rates, especially the structure of the rates charged to the final users of gas, that will determine the ultimate demand for gas. It is the people who will make the decisions to use somewhat more or somewhat less gas, to insulate or not to insulate, to wear warmer clothes or not, and these decisions will determine the amount of gas that is used. In the midst of the current serious natural gas shortage, rate structures of distribution and transmission companies still typically incorporate declining block rates (as the buyer uses more gas, he pays less per unit) and provide volume discounts to large users.

The importance of the rate structure issue is reflected in the interest shown by the Environmental Defense Fund (EDF). The EDF, which according to the public image spends much of its time lying down in front of bulldozers in order to stop energy projects, is in actuality genuinely interested in natural gas distribution rate structure. Early in its history and before the OPEC embargo, the EDF held a series of policy meetings at which economists played a central role. The

dominant thrust of the policy that was arrived at was that EDF
has a unique role to play on the demand side of the energy
problem. EDF found it difficult in the early 1970s, and finds
it even more difficult today, to choose between the various
supply alternatives in terms of their environmental harm.
Looking at the growth trend that prevailed during the 1960s,
EDF felt it absolutely essential to examine closely the increasing demand for energy in order to help determine a responsible
energy policy that would protect the environment.

The first manifestation of these concerns occurred in the
area of electric utilities. After considerable research, EDF
determined that there were possibilities for reforms of electric
utility rate structures in the direction of peak load pricing.
These reforms would tend to reduce the necessity of adding new
generating capacity to electric utility systems. Arguments
were presented before a number of state utility commissions,
and, in the historic *Madison Gas and Electric* case before the
Wisconsin Public Service Commission, EDF succeeded in having
the commission adopt, in principle, the notion of marginal
cost pricing and a program for the implementation of peak load
pricing. Somewhat later, EDF focused on the unusual natural
gas problem in the U.S. economy, which threatened industry
with natural gas curtailments, exposed consumers to higher and
higher prices, and created a real threat to the environment
because natural gas was being used inefficiently and was being
replaced by less clean fuels. EDF determined that there was a
basic dilemma due to the enormous gap between the prices
consumers were paying for natural gas and the marginal cost of
new natural gas supplies.

COST STRUCTURE OF NATURAL GAS SUPPLIES

Regardless of what happens to wellhead prices, the
distribution of natural gas is a natural monopoly, and distribution utulity rates and rate structures will continue to be
regulated in at least the foreseeable future. It is vitally
important that they be regulated in an intelligent way, which
means that attention must be paid to the marginal cost of gas.

In analyzing the gas industry, there are basically two
categories of costs. Unfortunately, they tend to point in
opposite and therefore confusing directions. Gas itself has a
low average cost because of the enormous amount of gas still
sold at very low prices under long-term contracts despite the
high marginal cost associated with adding new sources of supply.
In 1977 some gas still flowed at approximately 20¢/Mcf (about
one million Btu). This is a Btu-equivalent gasoline price of
3¢ to 5¢ per gallon--extremely low cost energy. Simultaneously,
new gas was being added or being proposed to be added to the
same transmission system at costs of $4 to $5/Mcf. Thus,
a factor of 20 or 25 separates the costs of some of the lowest
cost gas and the most expensive new gas supplements.

There are three basic technologies for adding supplemental or "exotic" gas. One is liquefied natural gas (LNG), which involves liquefying gas (usually from Algeria or Indonesia), importing it, and transforming it back into gaseous form. A second is synthetic natural gas (SNG), produced from petroleum or petroleum products. Basically, its production involves converting certain petroleum products (usually naphtha or propane) into natural gas. Because of the high marginal cost of petroleum to the U.S. economy, this source of gas is very expensive. The third technology, which is being examined by the industry, is the conversion of coal to natural gas. All of these supplemental sources seem to be somewhere between $3.50 and $5.00/Mcf. Some LNG is now coming into the system below that cost because the relevant contracts were signed before the OPEC price action; new LNG now being contracted for, however, will probably enter the system at costs of between $3.50 and $5.00/Mcf.

All of these supplements are much more expensive than historic flowing gas prices. Before Order 770 of the Federal Power Commission (FPC), the highest price a domestic producer could get for "new" gas in the interstate market was 50¢ to 60¢/Mcf. The average price that industrial users paid for direct purchases from pipelines was $0.90 to $1.10/Mcf as late as November 1976, according to Federal Power Commission data. This price reflected an increase of 40 percent within the preceding 12 months. We are thus dealing with an extremely complicated cost function. There is an enormous gap between average costs (and therefore prices) and the marginal cost of new gas supplies. There is discontinuity in the supply curve. Depending on what happens to President Carter's energy plan, we are likely to have a price for new gas produced conventionally by natural gas producers of around $1.75/Mcf. The next price at which gas can be bought at all will likely be around $3.50/Mcf, which is the lowest price that gas from exotic sources can be attained. These figures produce a very strange supply curve.

The problem is further complicated by the fact that there is another important set of costs associated with natural gas-- the imbedded costs of the pipeline and distribution system. The problem is unusually perplexing because just as there are low average costs and extremely high marginal costs associated with the gas itself, there are high embedded costs and extremely low marginal costs associated with additional use of the pipeline and distribution system. Although it is not universally the case, it is generally true that there is over-capacity in this system, which means that in most parts of the country the cost of adding to the transmission and distribution system caused by somewhat more natural gas flowing through the pipeline is close to zero. However, the fact that these marginal costs are close to zero does not mean that the pipeline and distribution companies do not have substantial revenue requirements

associated with discharging their investments in capacity. A
recent FPC document indicates that roughly $11 billion a year
has to be spent on the carrying costs of the pipeline and
distribution system. The United States uses roughly 20 billion
Mcf (or 20 quadrillion Btus) of natural gas a year, so the
average capital cost of the pipeline and distribution system
per thousand cubic feet is roughly 55¢. This can be a mislead-
ing figure because of the enormous regional variation in the
natural gas market (discussed below).

PECULIARITIES OF THE NATURAL GAS MARKET

There are a number of other factors that increase the
complexity of the natural gas market. One important and
complicating characteristic of the gas market is the weather
sensitivity of demand. Because of the intensity of use of
natural gas for heating, the market is extremely weather sensi-
tive, as we learned during the winter of 1976-1977. It is
important to design a rate structure that allows the distribution and transmission utility to avoid extreme fluctuations in
revenue due to weather. During the winter of 1976-1977, one
of the serious problems in some parts of the country was that,
owing to the unusually cold weather, more gas than usual was
sold to residential users and less than usual was sold to industrial users (increased residential sales resulted in industrial curtailments). Because residential rates are higher
than industrial rates, this replacement of industrial sales
with residential sales resulted in excess revenues for some
distribution companies. Thus, some of the companies--for
example, Rochester Gas and Electric--sent per capita rebates
to their customers. The opposite effect (deficient revenues),
of course, can occur under the existing rate structure when
there are unusually warm winters.

A second characteristic of the natural gas market that
makes the intelligent resolution of gas pricing absolutely
essential to a sound national energy policy is the close relationship between gas and oil. Regardless of what national
energy policy is adopted, the American energy market is going
to be increasingly characterized by the replacement of natural
gas by OPEC oil. This occurs basically in three ways. First,
curtailed industrial customers deprived of natural gas because
of shortages tend to switch to oil. Second, I have heard
rumors that, in some parts of the country, residential users
of natural gas are switching to oil. This is not impossible
considering the rates being charged for natural gas in New
England and New York state. Third, the gas supply option that
has the shortest lead time associated with it is petroleum
conversion. The quickest way to put more gas in the pipeline
is to turn petroleum products into gas; LNG and coal gasification have much longer lead times. Natural gas distribution
utilities are endeavoring to obtain permission from the

Department of Energy to build more petroleum conversion plants. Thus, the increased demand for natural gas or the failure to use gas efficiently quickly results in increased use of petroleum because of the various switching capabilities. In addition, LNG involves problems of balance of payments and national security similar to those created by imports of OPEC oil, because the source of the liquefied natural gas is also OPEC countries.

A third characteristic of the natural gas market is the enormously wasteful use of natural gas. In light of the marginal cost of new gas supplies, pilot lights may make sense when natural gas costs 20¢/Mcf, but they do not make much sense at $4.50/Mcf. Studies of the residential, industrial, and commercial use of natural gas, the efficiency of furnaces, the size of flues in furnaces, and the levels of insulation in homes and businesses that are heated with natural gas all indicate that there exist enormous possibilities to save natural gas. These studies conclude that consumption can be substantially reduced and still produce the same end-use consumer amenities. Many of these saving measures are consistent with a cost of natural gas of $1.50 to $2.00/Mcf; that is, one can "buy" natural gas by insulating homes of natural gas users for $1.50 to $2.00/Mcf, whereas new natural gas--from petroleum conversion, LNG (and therefore from OPEC), or from coal--costs from $3.50 to $5.00/Mcf.

A fourth characteristic of the natural gas market is enormous regional variation in price. Due to a variety of factors, it is partially caused by the method of allocating the costs of the pipeline between different distribution utilities. It is also due to the fact that some distribution utilities have excess capacity and are spreading their fixed costs over a declining number of sales units and therefore have to charge high rates. Another key cause is the fact that different supply sources are linked to different parts of the distribution system. In New England and New York state, the prices are so high that the market may very well be close to clearing. In other parts of the country, industrial users, for example, are paying as low as 70¢ to 80¢/Mcf for natural gas. It is therefore not very useful to look at national average prices. The average residential user in the United States is paying about $2.00/Mcf for natural gas, but this $2.00 reflects an enormous regional variation--around $4 in New England and around $1 in many other areas.

ROLLED-IN PRICING

The pattern for pricing new sources of natural gas has generally been to roll in the costs of the new gas with the costs of the gas already flowing and to charge consumers an average price. This has generally been advocated by the pipeline and distribution companies. Their position may be motivated

in part by a desire to use efficiently the existing pipeline
and transmission capacity by putting more gas into the pipelines. This uniformly priced gas is then sold by distribution
utilities under rate structures that generally feature volume
discounts, declining block rates, and high "demand" or "customer charges"--the charges for simply being a customer of the
company and using no gas. (The phrase "demand charge" has a
very different meaning when used in connection with electricity.)
These rate structures are justified by accounting formulas for
allocating the fixed costs of the pipeline and distribution
system and the operating costs (billing, maintenance, etc.)
associated with the system. These formulas, with considerable
justification, allocate a proportionally higher amount of these
costs to small users--to reflect the higher costs per unit of
gas sold due to billing, delivering gas, metering, and otherwise servicing small customers. Gas itself comes to the distribution utility at a relatively low and uniform rolled-in
price, and its costs are allocated accordingly.

A scientist at EDF has recently identified what might be
a serious problem associated with rolled-in pricing in this
context. I will refer to this problem as the "Habicht spiral"
after Ernst Habicht, who is the director of EDF's energy
program and who has examined these problems in some depth.
Another phrase that describes the problem is "backing into
expensive gas." And yet a third characterization of this
possible phenomenon is "the spectre of the self-defeating
rate increase."

The real danger associated with rolling in expensive new
sources of natural gas stems from the rate structures currently
used. Residential users generally pay more than industrial
users, while industrial users have a higher level of elasticity
associated with their demand for natural gas. This is largely
due to their ability to switch to other fields. If expensive
new gas is rolled in and prices are driven higher by putting
$4.00 or $5.00 gas into the pipeline and averaging it in, we
may some day approach the point (having already added a good
deal of exotic gas from petroleum, coal, or LNG to the pipeline) at which industrial rates reach $2.75 or $3.00/Mcf. Of
course, by this time residential rates will be $3.75 to $4.00/Mcf.
At that point there is a possible danger that the market might
clear. The industrial users of gas might decide that it is
better to use propane or some other energy source rather than
gas at that price and then switch, leaving the residential
users on the pipeline. There would thus be a decreasing number
of sales units over which to spread the fixed cost of the pipeline and distribution system, plus the high capital cost of LNG
and/or coal gasification plants. We might then experience the
reinforcing spiral of requirements of rate increases due to a
decreasing number of sales units over which fixed cost must be
spread. Reduced consumption in response to rate increases due
to the ability of industrial users to switch to other fuels

would require further increases in rates and ultimately could produce a self-reinforcing downward spiral. Looking at the markets in some parts of the country, this is not impossible even within the relatively short period (five to seven years). In the long term, I consider it to be a serious danger that must be borne in mind if rolled-in pricing is to be continued.

APPLICATION OF MARGINAL COST PRICING

The application of marginal cost pricing in this never-never land of natural gas--a world of discontinuous supply curves, weather-sensitive demand functions, and layers of federal and state regulations--is not an easy task. A number of problems including fairness, administrative difficulty, and political acceptability must be confronted. Probably the most perplexing problem that the implementation of marginal cost pricing would raise is the excess revenue problem. The pricing of every unit of gas at marginal cost (the $4.00 or $5.00 cost represented by new gas that is being added to the system) would result in excess revenue for the transmission and distribution utilities. These companies are regulated utilities and are thus limited to a fair rate of return. In the future, however, excess revenue may become less of a problem. If the sale of natural gas continues to decline, then the revenue requirements per one thousand cubic feet of the transmission and distribution utilities would go up as fixed costs are discharged over declining sales units. In the short term, however, the marginal cost pricing of natural gas raises the excess revenue problem in many parts of the country. This presents the difficulty of devising a mechanism for returning the "economic rent," represented by the difference between the marginal cost of gas and the allowed rate of return to the utility, to the consumers. This must be accomplished in some administratively feasible way that will also protect the revenue stability of the distribution and transmission utility.

A number of solutions are currently being discussed. One phrase that frequently appears in the relevant literature is "incremental pricing." This term is sometimes used interchangeably with "marginal cost pricing," but at other times it refers to something different and thus there is considerable confusion. I am using "incremental pricing" to describe proposals under which low priority users who are subject to curtailment (which they are anxious to avoid) are charged the full price for supplemental gas instead of the substantially lower rolled-in or average price. This approach has been debated recently before the Federal Energy Regulatory Commission with respect to liquefied natural gas. There has been an ongoing debate as to whether it should be applied to gas supplies produced from coal and petroleum; there has also been a debate as to whether it should be applied to the new definition of "new natural gas" being proposed in the Carter Administration's national energy plan.

A second set of proposals call for what might be referred to as "inverted rates." This is simply the opposite of declining block rates. There are a variety of ways in which inverted rates can be structured. One way would be to give every customer a percentage of his historic use of natural gas at a relatively cheap price and then charge a much higher price on the basis of marginal cost for the gas used in excess of that percentage. Depending on how it is administered, the implementation of an inverted rates structure may give rise to some severe problems. For example, calculating historic use and making adjustments for changes in the weather may be very difficult. If the base year used for determining historic use is a warm year and it is cold during the next year, customers may be confronted with a much higher bill in the second year. Instead, if the historic use year is a cold year and the next year is a warm year, the utility may not be able to earn its allowed rate of return.

Another way of establishing inverted rates is to provide each customer with a certain amount of gas (regardless of the customer's historic use) at a cheap price and then charge a price close to the marginal cost for the gas used in excess of that amount. A third mechanism is simply to provide lump sum rebates to each customer on the system. The national energy plan proposed by the Carter Administration contains a fourth mechanism, which would affect prices paid by end users of natural gas. This is part of the coal conversion program--in order to encourage users of natural gas to switch to coal, certain industrial and utility users capable of switching fuels would be taxed on their natural gas purchases to the extent that the after-tax price would be roughly equivalent to the price of refined oil substitutes for natural gas. Yet another mechanism that has been applied in some parts of the country is "flat rates" for natural gas. This is simply charging every one thousand cubic feet at the same price. Washington Gas Light Company, which has adopted this method, charges every user of natural gas roughly 20¢/therm or $2.00/Mcf for all gas used. (However, flat rates are combined with an $8.00/month customer charge.) One last mechanism that has been suggested is giving existing users tradeable entitlements in natural gas that can be sold to other customers. This would ultimately lead the price of natural gas to approach the opportunity cost of individual consumers.

Having analyzed these mechanisms, the market, and the difficulties involved in obtaining a practical solution, we will briefly discuss some of the proposals that seem to make the most sense under these circumstances. First, the benchmark or the signal for users to buy more or less natural gas should be the opportunity cost of gas. If the opportunity cost were pegged to each customer's ability to switch fuels or to conserve fuel, it would, of course, dictate different prices for different customers. Thus, it is preferable to use a market clearing price, one that would clear the market for natural gas as well as allow new residential and other hookups to be added. This price would be in the range of the Btu-equivalent delivered price of refined petroleum substitutes for natural gas.

We do not believe that in the real world the price should be precisely pegged to the cost of the various "exotic" supplements. Some of these supplements have been added because of the peculiar nature of the gas market. Some have high variable costs (e.g., petroleum conversion). Others have higher fixed costs and lower variable costs. If the supplement is already on line, then the relevant marginal cost element is the variable cost of the supplement. For example, the running cost of a petroleum conversion plant can be high because of the naptha or propane that is used as feedstock. Only if the supplement is not yet on line is marginal cost pricing relevant to the decision of whether to add the supplement.

The price that the opportunity cost benchmark produces should appear in the tailblocks of residential rate structures. Some form of inverted rates structure based on either historic use or on a given minimal amount of gas at a cheap price should be adopted by most distribution utilities. The residential user who must decide whether to insulate, whether to turn his thermostat down, or whether to retrofit his furnace is then confronted with a price at his margin of use that reflects the marginal or opportunity cost of gas. It is not necessary, however, to raise residential bills so that every unit of gas is sold at this price. With respect to industrial and commercial users, it is probably preferable to charge this price for all units of gas sold rather than simply in the tailblocks. This is because the incentive to switch to another fuel can only be captured by charging for all units of gas sold rather than simply in the tailblock. The target--the market clearing price--would not only be used for determining the rate structure for gas sold to existing consumers; it would also be the yardstick used to determine the desirability of new end uses of gas as well as new sources of gas supply. New hookups of natural gas would become possible if we achieve a market clearing price and should be allowed at the market clearing price. Since new users have the opportunity to choose among different fuels, they should pay the target price for all the gas they consume, not merely the gas consumed in their tailblocks. New gas from coal gasification plants or LNG should not be added to the system unless it can be delivered at or below this target price.

As noted above, the severe problem of revenue stability for the industry has been caused by the weather sensitivity of demand. The marginal cost pricing system described above would tend to alleviate that problem. The variation in sales in warm and cold winters would occur in the tailblocks of residential users. More of the expensive gas in the residential tailblocks would be sold in a cold winter and less of it would be sold in a warm winter. When less is sold during a warm winter, it can instead be sold to industrial users who might otherwise be interrupted or curtailed, and it would be sold at the same price that it would have been sold at in the residential tailblock. Thus, the problem of disparity between residential and industrial prices and, therefore, the wide fluctuations of utility revenue depending on whether it is a cold or a warm winter would be alleviated. In a cold winter some industrial sales of high-priced gas (based on marginal cost) would be lost, but sales in residential tailblocks that would tend to be at these high prices would be added.

Let us now turn to a problem associated with natural gas pricing and the United States' relationship with OPEC. This problem may be expected to persist in the natural gas area as well as in a number of other areas until rational pricing for oil is achieved. There is an argument that the United States should underprice or in some other way encourage consumers to use gas produced from coal gasification plants in order to prevent them from switching to oil that must be imported. A true marginal cost pricing system for gas might reduce the viability of coal gasification and, at least in the short term, cause OPEC oil to replace gas produced from coal. Although this is troubling, there appears to be a clear solution. The problem arises because we are not charging the right price for OPEC oil. If, indeed, there are additional costs associated with the increased use of OPEC oil, then the price charged should reflect these costs. Only then will Americans be able to make rational decisions regarding their consumption of oil.

Another aspect of marginal cost pricing that needs to be examined is the case of expensive gas supplements that are already on line. Suppose that the market clearing price is $2.75/Mcf and that there is a petroleum conversion plant on a distribution utility system that is producing gas at a variable cost of $3.50/Mcf. This is not unlikely, given the high cost of petroleum feedstocks. The usual solution would be to raise the market clearing price by taking that plant out of operation. We should not be producing gas at $3.50 variable cost and selling it at $2.75. If we are able to raise the price to $2.85 to reduce demand to such a level that we can take that plant out of operation, that would be the preferred solution. Some supplements already on line have lower variable costs. The deciding factor for whether the price should be raised to take plants off the line should be the variable cost.

If we look toward the future, we come back to the problem dealt with at the beginning of this chapter--that of allocating transmission and distribution expenses. This problem has not been sufficiently handled in most pricing analysis documents with which I am familiar. It is an extremely difficult problem, and the analysis of it leads one in exactly the opposite

direction than does the analysis for allocating the expenses
of the gas itself. In most parts of the country, marginal
costs of transmission and distribution are extremely low,
whereas embedded costs tend to be higher. This would argue
that we allocate transmission and distribution expenses in a
fashion that is exactly the opposite of the way in which we
allocate the cost of gas. That is, we charge the highest
price for transmission and distribution to the customers with
the least elastic demand for gas. In looking at a distribution
or transmission utility and devising a rate structure that
leads to an appropriate rate of return and at the same time
gives an economically justifiable price for gas, transmission
and distribution expenses are probably useful in taking up part
of the gap between the average price of flowing gas and the
market clearing price or the price of new natural gas entering
the system. Applying the "inverse elasticity rule" temporally,
not merely across customer classes, there appears to be a strong
marginal cost argument for allowing higher rates of depreciation
to transmission and distribution utilities. Thus, the utilities
can recover the embedded costs of transmission and distribution
during the time period in which there is the least price elasticity. This "time of lowest price elasticity" may be the
present because the market clearing price for gas exceeds the
average cost of flowing gas by an enormous amount. In general,
I believe that these expenses can be used to help derive a set
of rates and a rate structure that guarantees a fair rate of
return and at the same time is able to bring prices in the
tailblocks and to the large users of gas closer to their
marginal cost levels.

COMPARISON OF TYPICAL RATE STRUCTURE
WITH MARGINAL COST RATE STRUCTURE (10 ccf = 1 Mcf)

A. Typical rate structure
    1. Residential
    Customer charge--$4.50/month
          first 20 ccf--25¢/ccf
          next 80 ccf--22¢/ccf
          next 300 ccf--20¢/ccf
          additional ccf--16¢/ccf

    2. Industrial
    Customer charge--$25.00/month
          first 100 Mcf--15¢/ccf
          additional use--12¢/ccf

B. Marginal cost rate structure
    (assume substitute fuel price = 24¢/ccf)
    1. Residential
    Customer charge = 0
    Gas charge
    ● for first 50% of weather-adjusted historic use--
      8¢/ccf
    ● for next 25% of weather-adjusted historic use--
      16¢/ccf
    ● for use of gas in excess of 75% of weather-
      adjusted historic use--24¢/ccf

    2. New residential
    Customers must pay hook-up costs (either in a flat
    payment or in installments)
    Gas charge for all units--24¢/ccf

    3. Industrial
    Customer charge = 0
    All units of gas--24¢/ccf or, alternatively,
        a. rates for industrial customers capable of fuel
           switching and for new industrial customers--
           24¢/ccf
        b. rates for existing industrial customers incapable
           of fuel switching [same as (1) above; rates based
           on historic use for residential consumers]

APPENDIX B

DECISION RULES CONCERNING NEW SUPPLY OPTIONS

Option A: To add new supply at a cost of 32¢/ccf.

Response: Assuming the market clears at 24¢/ccf, do not add
the supply.
Assuming the market clears (with no new hook-ups
allowed) at 24¢/ccf, offer new hook-ups at 32¢/ccf.

Option B: To add new supply at a cost of 21¢/ccf.
Response: Add the supply; if an open-ended amount of gas can
be obtained at 21¢/ccf, reduce the tailblock price,
the price to new users, and the price to industrial
users from 24¢ to 21¢/ccf.

5
Evaluation of the New Mexico Public Utility Rate Indexing Experiment

Alfred L. Parker

INTRODUCTION

In March 1975, the New Mexico Public Service Commission (NMPSC) announced the acceptance of the Cost of Service Index (CSI) approach to setting electric service rates. The commission's decision and order adopting the CSI on a trial basis was issued on April 22, 1975.[1] The acceptance of this unique approach to public utility regulation was in response to the financial crises in the electric utility industry in the early 1970s and in recognition of the significant problems associated with the traditional rate proceeding.

Problems with the traditional rate hearing had been amply demonstrated in the case filed on December 20, 1973, by the Public Service Company of New Mexico (PNM). The hearings of this rate proceeding generated more than 3,000 pages of testimony over a 90-day period. Almost ten months passed before the NMPSC granted an overall increase of 6.5584 percent in base rates--well below the 15 percent increase requested by PNM. Dissatisfied with the order, PNM entered an appeal in the District Court, thus further extending the rate proceeding.

Recognizing that this case was the first of what promised to be a continuing series of rate cases resulting from continuing inflation and planned major expansion in the company's facilities, the NMPSC chose to try the CSI approach. It was suggested that regulatory lag associated with the traditional rate proceeding would discourage potential investors and significantly increase PNM's cost of capital required for projected expansion.[2] Thus it was argued that the continuation of the traditional rate proceeding would both increase the cost of service to the consumer and limit the ability of the utility to provide that service.

The CSI was in fact designed to accomplish four primary goals:
1. cope with regulatory lag
2. minimize revenue requirements
3. encourage company efficiency
4. promote regulatory efficiency.[3]

97

TABLE 1.   COST OF SERVICE INDEX REPORT, DECEMBER 31, 1976

Part I.   Jurisdictional electric investment

1. Total PNM electric investment $ 399,687,006
2. Jurisdictional electric investment
   allocation factor   0.89366
3. Jurisdictional electric investment
   (line 1 x 2) $ 357,184,289

Part II. Jurisdictional electric common equity

4. Common equity (monthly average) $ 146,314,498
5. Nonutility investments $ 5,262,785
6. Jurisdictional capital allocation factor   0.84362
7. Jurisdictional electric common equity
   [(line 4 - 5) x 6] $ 118,994,046
8. First preceding jurisdictional electric
   common equity investment $ 104,057,695
9. Second preceding jurisdictional electric
   common equity investment $ 102,642,888
10. Third preceding jurisdictional electric
    common equity investment $ 96,865,513
11. Average jurisdictional electric common
    equity investment [(lines 7 + 8 + 9 + 10)
    ÷ 4] $ 105,640,036

Part III. Jurisdictional electric net income
           available for common equity

12. Jurisdictional electric operating revenue $ 86,274,171
13. Electric expenses other than income tax $ 64,218,946
14. Jurisdictional expense allocation factor   0.86199
15. Jurisdictional expenses other than
    income tax (line 13 x 14) $ 55,356,089

98

16. Jurisdictional income tax $ 8,186,684

17. Net jurisdictional electric operating income [line 12 − (15 + 16)] $ 22,731,398

18. Electric allowance for funds during construction (AFDC) $ 5,762,917

19. Jurisdictional AFDC (line 18 x 2) $ 5,150,088

20. Income adjustment for preceding calculation $ 304,263

21. Total interest expense and preferred dividends $ 17,863,918

22. Jurisdictional interest expense and preferred dividends (line 21 x 6) $ 15,070,359

23. Jurisdictional net income available for common equity [(line 17 + 19 + 20) − 22] $ 13,115,390

Part IV. Return on jurisdictional common equity

24. Annual return on jurisdictional common equity (ROE) (line 23 − 11)   12.415%

25. Percentage difference between current ROE and 13.5% − 14.5%   1.085%

26. Revenue differential [(line 11 x 25) ÷ 48.63%*] $ 2,356,962

27. Jurisdictional kwh sales during period $2,967,600,959

28. Incremental index factor (line 26 ÷ 27) $ 0.000794/

29. Previous index factor $ 0.002209/

30. Current cost of service index (line 28 + 29) $ 0.003003/

*Effective tax rate for PNM.

Source: "Cost of Service Index report," December 31, 1976. Public Service Company of New Mexico, Electric Department.

99

At the time of this writing the New Mexico CSI has been in operation for more than two years. Thus it now appears appropriate to review the performance of this approach and, more specifically, to determine if the CSI has in fact succeeded in promoting the objectives listed above. First, however, it is necessary to have some basic understanding of the mechanics of the CSI. There are several unusual features of the New Mexico CSI that may significantly affect its usefulness as a means of providing a responsive regulatory process. These elements and the basic nature of the New Mexico CSI are explored in the following section.

THE COST OF SERVICE INDEX CLAUSE

The CSI requires a quarterly review of the investment, operating expenses, and revenues for electric service under the jurisdiction of the NMPSC. It provides for automatic quarterly adjustments in the base rates when the "jurisdictional net income available for common equity" provides a rate of return either above or below the allowed rate of return on such capital.

Table 1 provides a somewhat simplified version of the PNM "Cost of Service Index Report" for December 31, 1976. The actual report provides substantially greater detail, but the basic elements of the calculation remain. As indicated in line 24, the percentage return on jurisdictional common equity (ROE) is computed by dividing the jurisdictional net income available for common equity (line 23) by the average jurisdictional electric common equity investment (line 11). Line 23 has been adjusted upward to include that income that would have been received had the CSI in effect at the end of this reporting period been in effect during the entire 12-month period. In this report, the adjustment is $304,263 (line 21); thus, the resulting calculation "annual return on jurisdictional common equity" is a hypothetical or simulated ROE rather than the actual ROE. The hypothetical ROE indicates what would have been earned if the index factor in effect during this quarter had been in effect for the preceding 12 months. The hypothetical ROE, 12.415 percent (Table 1), is not within the 13.5 to 14.5 percent range; therefore, an adjustment in the CSI is automatically implemented.

The NMPSC, in its decision and order on case 1196, allowed the PNM to earn a ROE between 13.5 and 14.5 percent. More precisely, PNM's rate structure is permitted to generate enough revenue to cover the costs of preferred capital, debt capital, taxes, depreciation, operation, and maintenance and earn between 13.5 and 14.5 percent ROE. This allowable range of return on equity will not be changed except through a formal rate hearing.

In the calculations presented in Table 1, the CSI has been

adjusted upward to 0.003003/kwh in order to provide a hypothetical ROE for the preceding twelve months of 13.5 percent.
Under the provisions of the NMPSC order, the new CSI goes into
effect after a one-month delay--in this case February 1, 1977.
The one-month delay is, in effect, an annual four-month
regulatory lag. PNM knows that during these four months their
rates may or may not earn the allowable ROE. It should also
be emphasized that the CSI does not permit PNM to make up in
future reporting periods for a ROE below the allowable range.
Similarly, the CSI does not attempt to confiscate actual earnings in excess of the allowable range that may be earned during
a particular reporting period (discussed below).

The NMPSC decision and order requires that PNM's accounts
be audited by a certified public accountant retained by the
NMPSC. When the changes in costs have been verified, the
appropriate adjustment becomes effective after the one-month
delay from the last reporting date. The cost-of-fuel rate
adjustment clause (CFRAC) is not included as a part of the CSI,
and fuel costs are therefore excluded as a cost of service in
the calculations summarized in Table 1. Thus, base rates may
change as a result of changes in the cost of fuel, while costs
allowable to the CSI remain constant.

CSI's TWO YEARS OF OPERATION

The price adjustments resulting from the application of the
cost of service index over the past two years are summarized
in Figure 1. The NMPSC decision and order established a phase-
in period so that the first accounting period would cover
April 1 to June 30, 1975. The base rates for this period were
calculated to meet the costs of the 1973 test year. The ROE
at the end of this first reporting period was 8.8 percent.
Since no index factor was in operation in this period, actual
and hypothetical ROEs were both equal to 8.8 percent--well
below the allowed minimum of 13.5 percent.

On the basis of the data for this second quarter of 1975
only and after a one-month delay, the base rates were adjusted
upward on July 1 by $0.002688/kwh. The available data suggested
that this additional revenue, if collected in the first reporting period, would have raised the hypothetical ROE to 13.5
percent.

The second accounting period ended September 30, 1975.
The hypothetical ROE for the preceding six-month period was
calculated to be 15.74 percent, i.e., the PNM "Cost of Service
Index report" indicated that if the rate adjustment factor of
0.002688/kwh had been in effect for the entire six-month period,
that company would have earned a ROE of 15.74 percent. This
high hypothetical ROE resulted from the high load factor maintained by PNM during the third quarter of the year.

The actual ROE during the second reporting period (the
third quarter of the calendar year) was 12.55 percent. Rate

101

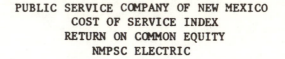

Figure 1

PUBLIC SERVICE COMPANY OF NEW MEXICO
COST OF SERVICE INDEX
RETURN ON COMMON EQUITY
NMPSC ELECTRIC

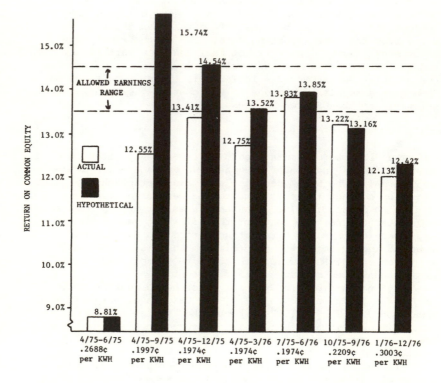

Source: Public Service Company of New Mexico, Cost of Service Index, NMPSC
Case No. 1330, Exhibit JDG-6.

adjustments, however, are based on the hypothetical ROE; thus, the rate level was lowered by $0.00691/kwh to $0.001997/ kwh effective November 1, 1975. This reduction was designed to bring the hypothetical ROE for the second accounting period to the upper limit of 14.5 percent.

The third reporting period ended December 31, 1975. PNM reported a hypothetical ROE of 14.54 percent, slightly above the allowable range. The actual ROE earned by PNM was reported to be 13.41 percent. Since the hypothetical ROE was above the allowable range, the index factor was again lowered after a one-month lag to 0.001974/kwh.

During the fourth reporting period ending March 31, 1976, the hypothetical ROE and actual ROE fell to 13.52 percent and 12.75 percent, respectively. Since the hypothetical ROE was within the allowable range, no adjustment in the index factor was required.

Similarly, the PNM Cost of Service Index report dated June 30, 1976, found the hypothetical ROE to be 13.85 percent, within the allowable range. The index factor of $0.001974/kwh thus remained in effect. The "Cost of Service Index reports" for September 1976 and December 1976 both projected hypothetical ROEs below the minimum 13.5 percent. The index factor was therefore adjusted upward to $0.002209/kwh effective November 1, 1976, and upward to $0.003003/kwh effective February 1, 1977.

An examination of the actual ROE reported for PNM in Figure 1 suggests that the application of the CSI has not guaranteed that PNM's actual ROE will remain within the 13.5 to 14.5 percent range. However, there is some indication that the CSI has tended to stabilize PNM's ROE. But what has been the effect of the CSI on PNM's cost of capital, its efficiency, and the efficiency of the New Mexico Public Service Commission?

CSI AND THE COST OF CAPITAL

Testimony presented in April 1977 by officers of PNM and expert witnesses in NMPSC case 1330 showed that both the cost of equity and the cost of debt have been favorably affected by the CSI.[4] In view of the 1977-1981 PNM construction budget, estimated at $946 million, it is clear that a reduction in the company's cost of capital would mean substantial dollar savings for New Mexico consumers.

Changes in the cost of equity capital have been reflected in the market price of PNM's stock. Available data appears to support the conclusion that the introduction of the CSI has had the effect of raising the market price of PNM stock. Table 2 shows the monthly closing stock prices for the first six months of 1975 of PNM and the average of 95 utilities, all of which are traded on the New York Stock Exchange. This data shows a significant increase in the price of PNM stock relative to the average of 95 utilities immediately following the announcement of the commission's acceptance of the CSI in early March 1975.

TABLE 2. AVERAGE OF 95 ELECTRIC UTILITIES,
MONTH-END CLOSING PRICES, JANUARY TO JUNE
1975

| | Month-end closing price | | Ratio of PNM/95 electric utilities |
	PNM	95 electric utilities	
January	$14.38	$16.66	0.86
February	14.00	16.61	0.84
March	15.75	16.21	0.97
April	16.75	15.94	1.05
May	18.25	16.97	1.08
June	20.38	18.67	1.09

Source: The Wall Street Journal, various issues. Public Service Company of New Mexico, Cost of Service Index, NMPSC Case 1330, exhibit JDG-1.

A similar pattern is shown in Figure 2, which shows the ratio of the month-end price of PNM stock to the month-end price of the Standard and Poor's index of 40 utility stocks. In March 1975, the price of PNM stock rose sharply relative to the Standard and Poor's Utility Stock Index. For the 17 months from March 1975 through July 1976 following the commission's acceptance of the CSI, PNM stock has been higher relative to the Standard and Poor's Stock Index than at any time in the preceding two years (since February 1973). On the average, the ratio of PNM stock to the Standard and Poor's Utility Stock Index was 15 percent higher in this 17-month period than it was in the two years preceding the commission's decision.[5]

While PNM's earnings per share did increase in the months following the commission's acceptance of the CSI, the data recorded in Figure 3 suggest that PNM's market price was not increasing solely because of improved earnings. Figure 3 compares the price/earnings (PE) ratios of PNM and the Standard and Poor's utilities for the period January 1973 through February 1977. The figure shows clearly that in the two years preceding the commission's decision, PNM's PE ratio was consistantly lower than the PE ratio of the Standard and Poor's utilities; however, in the 24 months from March 1975 through February 1977, the PE ratio for PNM has generally been higher than Standard and Poor's.[6]

The data we have examined clearly support the conclusion

Figure 2

RATIO OF MONTH-END PRICE OF
PUBLIC SERVICE COMPANY OF NEW MEXICO'S
STOCK TO MONTH-END PRICE OF STANDARD & POOR'S
UTILITIES STOCK PRICE INDEX

January 1973 - February 1977

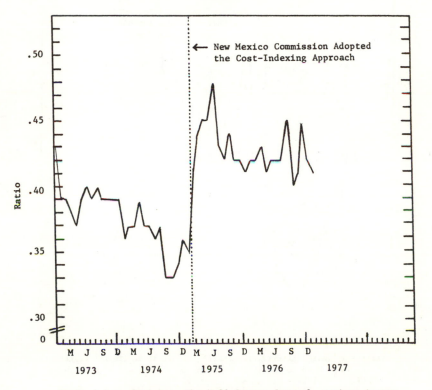

Derived from data in: The Wall Street Journal, various issues.
Standard & Poor's Corporation, Stock Guide, various issues;
Standard & Poor's Trade and Securities Statistics, Security Price
Index Record, 1974 Edition and Current Statistics, various issues.

Source: Public Service Company of New Mexico, Cost of Service
         Index, NMPSC Case No. 1330, Exhibit JDG-2.

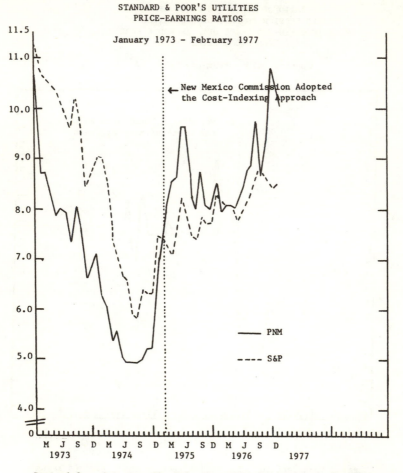

Figure 3

STANDARD & POOR'S UTILITIES
PRICE-EARNINGS RATIOS

January 1973 - February 1977

← New Mexico Commission Adopted
the Cost-Indexing Approach

——— PNM

- - - - S&P

Derived from data in: The Value Line FUNDAC Data Base. The Wall Street
Journal, various issues. Standard & Poor's Corporation, Stock Guide,
various issues; Standard & Poor's Trade and Securities Statistics,
Security Price Index Record, 1974 Edition and Current Statistics, various
issues.

Source: Public Service Company of New Mexico, Cost of Service Index,
NMPSC Case No. 1330, Exhibit JDG-3.

that the shift in the relative price of PNM stock is the result
of the commission's indexing decision itself rather than the
level of earnings that implementation of that decision has
created. The further inference is that the commission's indexing decision has resulted in a decline in the cost of equity
capital to PNM.[7]

While recognizing that the size of the shift in the
valuation of PNM stock cannot be measured with precision, PNM's
experts have constructed an estimate of the savings on the cost
of equity resulting from the CSI. This estimate was constructed
as follows.

> The various measures we have examined all indicate,
> holding other things equal, the price of PNM stock
> is now 10 to 20 percent greater than prior to the
> indexing decision. It would take an increase of
> approximately 10 to 20 percent in earnings per
> share to achieve a comparable gain in market price
> of the stock; such an increase in earnings is
> equivalent to a rise of 1 to 2 percentage points
> in return on equity.[8]

Using this estimate to determine the savings in the cost
of equity capital for PNM projects during 1976, we find that
they amounted to between $3.4 and $6.6 million and that the
annual cost of capital savings for 1981 are projected to be
between $13.2 and $26.5 million (see Table 3).

Evidence concerning the CSI's impact on the cost of debt
capital is more limited, but available data suggest that PNM's
cost of borrowing may have declined by more than one percentage
point as a consequence of the commission's decision. Although
PNM expert witnesses express somewhat less confidence in this
estimate of the savings on debt, the evidence does point to
some savings.[9]

To get some indication of how the indexing decision
affected PNM's cost of debt, the yields on PNM's outstanding
bonds have been compared with yields on other outstanding AA
utility bonds. Figure 4 illustrates one such comparison for
the years 1973 through 1976. This figure shows the differences
in yields between Standard and Poor's AA-rated utility bonds
and PNM's 7¼ percent bonds maturing in 1999. During 1974 there
was a sharp rise in the yields on PNM bonds, but yields appeared
to be back to normal by early 1975. The indexing decision
appears to have prompted no immediate change in PNM bond yields
relative to Standard and Poor's bond yields.

In the fall of 1975, PNM bond yields began to decline
relative to Standard and Poor's yields on AA bonds; during
1976 and continuing into 1977, PNM yields have been lower than
Standard and Poor's yields. A similar pattern of yields was
obtained when Standard and Poor's AA-rated utility bonds were
compared with PNM 8 1/8 percent bonds due in 2001 and PNM 5 7/8

TABLE 3. ANNUAL COST OF CAPITAL SAVINGS

I. Current annual savings

Common equity:

December 31, 1976	$155,774,000
Annual savings @ 1%	3,445,000*
@ 2%	6,590,100*

Long-term debt:

$9\frac{1}{8}$% series	25,000,000
Annual savings @ 1.2%	300,000
Total annual savings: $3,745,000 to $6,890,100	

II. 1981 annual savings ($1.0 billion expansion)

Equity:

$155.8 million plus 50% of	
$1.0 billion = $655,800,000	
Annual savings @ 1%	13,240,500*
@ 2%	26,481,000*

Debt:

$25 million plus 50% of	
$1.0 billion = 525,000,000	
Annual savings @ 1.2%	6,300,000
Total 1981 annual savings: $19,540,500 to $32,781,000	

*Tax rate of 50.47%.
Source: Public Service Company of New Mexico, Cost of Service
Index, NMPSC Case 1330, exhibit JDG-5.

percent bonds due in 1997.

A shift in relative yields on PNM bonds is evident. PNM
bonds were yielding approximately 20 basis points less than
Standard and Poor's bonds in 1976, having yielded 20 to 30
basis points more than Standard and Poor's bonds in 1973-1975.
This decline in the yield on PNM bonds of roughly 40 to 50 basis
points in relation to Standard and Poor's AA-rated bonds has
been attributed to the indexing decision and its application.

The estimate of the savings on the cost of debt described
above assumes that PNM retained its AA rating. Evidence has
been presented suggesting that in fact PNM would not have
retained its AA rating if the NMPSC had not accepted the CSI
when it did.[10] The average difference between AA- and A-rated
utility bonds is reported to be at least 70 basis points.[11]

PNM therefore estimates the total savings on the cost of
debt to be approximately 1.2 percent, i.e., 50 basis points
within the AA classification and 70 basis points between the
AA and A ratings. On the basis of this estimate of savings on

Figure 4

DIFFERENCE IN BOND YIELDS TO MATURITY
BETWEEN PUBLIC SERVICE COMPANY OF NEW MEXICO'S
FIRST MORTGAGE 7 1/4 PERCENT SERIES DUE 1999 AND
STANDARD & POOR'S AA RATED UTILITIES

January 1973 - January 1977

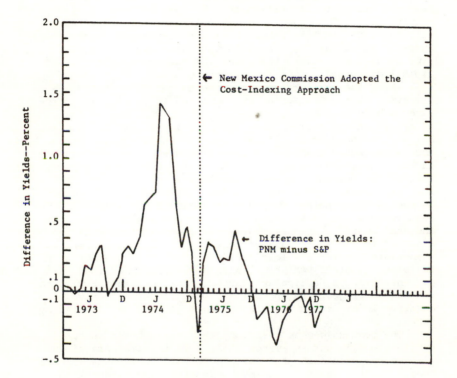

Derived from data in: Standard & Poor's Corporation, Bond Guide,
Bond Outlook and Fixed Income Investor, various issues.

Source: Public Service Company of New Mexico, Cost of Service
Index, NMPSC Case No. 1330, Exhibit JDG-4.

the cost of debt, PNM has testified that $300,000 was saved
on the cost of debt in 1976; PNM has also projected that
annual savings on the cost of debt will be approximately $6.3
million by 1981 (see Table 3).

While there may be reason to question the accuracy of
some of the estimates of savings on the cost of capital presented by PNM, there is little question that the CSI has a
potential for significant savings for the New Mexico consumer.

CSI AND COMPANY AND REGULATORY EFFICIENCY

In March 1975, Dr. Irwin Stelzer of National Economic
Research Associates testified that he "was bothered by the
possibility that management might get lazy without the spur
of regulatory lag."[12] Others have also expressed concern that
indexing would destroy the companies' incentive for efficiency,
thus perhaps offsetting the potential savings on the cost of
capital discussed in the preceding section.

There are in fact several elements unique to the construction of the New Mexico CSI designed to provide an incentive to hold costs down. For example, the CSI allows the rate
of return on the jurisdictional equity investment to be within
a 1 percent band around 14 percent. If PNM's hypothetical
ROE is projected to be below the allowable range, the index
factor will be adjusted to project a 13.5 ROE. The only way
for PNM to increase its ROE above that level is to operate
more efficiently.[13] As noted above, if PNM's rate of return
on equity falls below 13.5 percent during any one quarter, the
lost revenue cannot be recovered in succeeding quarters. In
the next quarter, the base rates (or index factor) will be
adjusted to provide a 13.5 percent return with no attempt to
compensate PNM for the loss during the previous quarter. On
the other hand, if PNM should earn a return higher than 14.5
percent during a particular quarter, the index factor will be
reduced to project the upper limit of 14.5 percent only. The
earnings in excess of the allowable range will be retained by
PNM.

The commission has described this arrangement as "a
double-edged incentive system where cost reducing practices
will be rewarded while the failure to hold down costs will be
penalized."[14] There is, however, insufficient evidence at
this time to determine if the 1 percent return range on common
equity provides adequate incentive for the promotion of company
efficiency.

The significance of this so-called double-edged incentive
is magnified by the required one-month delay between the
reporting date and the effective date of a new index factor.
Thus, earnings above or below the allowable range will continue
one month beyond their appearance in PNM's "Cost of Service
Index report." The one-month lag is, in effect, a four-month
annual regulatory lag. So while regulatory lag has been

significantly reduced by the CSI, it has not disappeared completely.

It has been argued that the use of the hypothetical ROE rather than actual ROE as the basis for the adjustment of the index factor tends to work in just the opposite direction, i.e., reducing the weight of this double-edged incentive for company efficiency.[15] It is suggested that use of the hypothetical ROE has the effect of overstating both "losses" and "profits." When the company's ROE is less than 13.5 percent, the deficiency tends to be overstated, and when the company's ROE is more than 14.5 percent, the excess profits tend to be overstated by this approach. Therefore, the adjustment in the base rates (or index factor) to compensate for the excess profit or the deficiency in earnings will be larger than if the adjustments were based on actual ROE.

This seems to suggest that excess earnings in one quarter resulting from increased efficiency may be at least partially confiscated by an excessive downward adjustment in the index factor, and similarly, that a deficiency in earnings in one quarter may be partially offset by an exaggerated increase in the index factor. PNM's experience during 1975 and 1976, as indicated in Figure 1, does not support this general conclusion. While such an overstatement is possible (as in reporting period October 1975 to September 1976), the hypothetical ROE has much more frequently understated rather than overstated losses. The use of the hypothetical ROE therefore appears to have increased the weight of the double-edged incentive for efficiency.

Over the two years we have studied PNM's actual ROE, with the exception of the second quarter of 1976, it has been below the minimum level permitted by the commission's decision and order--13.5 percent. During this period, company incentives to reduce costs should therefore have been more than adequate as they attempted to provide investors with a return on equity equal to or greater than that available on alternative investments with comparable risks.

Whether existing incentives for company efficiency will continue to be adequate in the near future is of course difficult to predict. This uncertainty clearly increases the importance of NMPSC efforts to develop effective measures of company efficiency. An important advantage attributed to the use of the CSI is that by freeing the commission from the traditional rate hearing, the staff has more time to pursue its other regulatory responsibilities--such as prior certification of new plant construction and new securities, the review of rate structures, and more. The NMPSC has over the past two years devoted at least a portion of this time to the development of measures of company efficiency.[16] The traditional rate proceeding is expensive and time-consuming for both the regulated utility and the commission. When so occupied, the commission, with its limited resources, is forced to neglect other regulatory functions. Thus, it is certainly possible that in the long run, the freeing of commission resources from the rate-case cycle may increase the effectiveness of the commission in its pursuit of reliable service and reasonable prices for New Mexico consumers and a "fair return" for investors.

It is argued that the CSI similarly contributes to company efficiency by freeing PNM resources from the rate-case cycle. These resources may then be available to solve other problems, thus contributing to greater efficiency of the utility and lower costs for its customers. In recent testimony, PNM listed a number of important programs, and, according to PNM, some of these would not be in existence without indexing. This list included programs designed to assure reliable sources of electricity at reasonable cost (the proposal for a Solar Hybrid Repowering Program) and programs designed to improve customer utilization of electric service (the design and implementation of time-of-day rates for some PNM customers).

Any dollar estimate of the savings that have resulted or may result from increased company and/or commission efficiency would at best be highly speculative at this time. However, the impact may become more visible as PNM continues to operate under this unique regulatory arrangement.

SUMMARY AND CONCLUSIONS

The New Mexico cost of service index has been in operation since April, 1975. This unique experiment represents a sub-stantial departure from the traditional regulatory process. The CSI was designed to reduce regulatory lag to a reasonable period, to minimize revenue requirements of the utility, to promote efficiency in all areas of company operation, and to improve the ability of the regulatory commission to regulate efficiently.

Although evidence of the CSI's performance in each of these areas is limited owing to the relatively short life of the experiment, there are some indicators that suggest that the CSI is in fact performing well. The data and analysis presented in this chapter support the following conclusions with respect to the application of this concept:

- The CSI has increased and tended to stabilize PNM's return on equity.
- The effect of the CSI on the cost of equity and the cost of debt capital appears to be in the direction of significant savings.
- The CSI appears to have improved PNM's ability to attract the large investment required to meet its 1977-1981 construction budget.

In addition, the analysis presented here suggests that the effect of the CSI on company and regulatory efficiency may be important in promoting reliable service at reasonable

112

rates and efficient utilization of electric service by consumers. Although we are now unable to quantify these effects,
their potential importance is great indeed.

The limited experience with the CSI concept--and the
even more limited hard evidence of its impact on the regulated
utility, the regulatory commission, and the consumer--suggests
it is clearly too early to declare the concept a success or a
failure. There does appear to be sufficient encouragement to
warrant a continuation of the experiment. Because there will
be some severe tests of this concept in the near future, a
program for continuous monitoring and periodic formal review
is appropriate.

NOTES

1. State of New Mexico Public Service Commission,
Decision and order, Public Service Company of New Mexico Case
1196, Santa Fe, New Mexico (April 22, 1975). Represented in
Public Utility Reports, 1975, 4th series, vol. 8.

2. Albert J. Robison, "The New Mexico Cost of Service
Index." Iowa State Regulatory Conference, May 20, 1976, p. 2.

3. *Ibid.,* p. 4.

4. Public Service Company of New Mexico, Cost of Service
Index, NMPSC Case no. 1330. Testimony of Gerry D. Geist,
Irwin M. Stelzer, and Eugene W. Meyer.

5. Herman G. Roseman, "The Cost of Service Adjustment
Clause and the Cost of Capital of Public Service Company of
New Mexico." National Economic Research Associates, Inc.,
mimeograph, p. 4.

6. *Ibid.,* p. 5-6.

7. *Ibid.,* p. 6-7. "This follows because investors now
appear to put a higher value on a dollar of PNM earnings than
they did before the indexing decision." Footnote, p. 7.

8. *Ibid.,* p. 9.

9. *Ibid.,* p. 9.

10. Public Service Company of New Mexico, Cost of Service
Index, NMPSC Case no. 1330, Testimony of Gerry D. Geist, p. 4.

11. *Ibid.*

12. Public Service Company of New Mexico, Cost of Service,
NMPSC Case no. 1330, Testimony of Irwin M. Stelzer, p. 2.

13. Transcript of hearing before the New Mexico Public
Service Commission in the matter of a rate filing by Public
Service Company of New Mexico, Case 1196 (March 5, 6, 1975),
p. 67.

14. Decision and order before the New Mexico Public
Service Commission in the matter of a rate filing by Public
Service Company of New Mexico, Case 1196 (April 22, 1975),
p. 16.

15. Transcript of hearing, Case 1196, p. 165; W. David
Eberle, master's thesis, University of New Mexico, December
1976, p. 65-66.

16. The NMPSC staff is continuing its efforts to develop
effective measures of electric utility efficiency as of this
date. Their approach has been directed at the development of
attainable standards for labor cost per kilowatt hour and
also capital, materials, and fuel cost per kilowatt hour.
Intraindustry comparisons of the resulting ratios are also
being examined as potential indicators of changes in company
efficiency.

6
Procedural Impediments to Optimal Rate Making

Thomas D. Morgan

PROCEDURAL IMPEDIMENTS

As a lawyer, I recognize that the legal profession has contributed in no small way to the problems experienced in the regulation of public utilities in recent years. Yet I believe that the profession is coming to recognize the problems and to develop some consensus that changes are required. Contrary to some popular myths, lawyers do not always try to foul things up. In many ways, we are like Charlie Brown saying, "How can we do so badly when we are so sincere?"

I believe that most of the procedural delays and related problems of rate-making procedure can be traced to three main causes. First, lawyers have assumed that public utility rate cases are like any other cases. If the trial process works well to decide whether John wronged Bill, it should serve equally well to decide the rate of return allowed the local electric company. It seems to me that in equating the situations we simply have been wrong. Even assuming the trial process does the traditional jobs well--an assumption undergoing serious reexamination today--traditional legal procedures work best in the dissection of past events. While rate cases inevitably involve great attention to past facts, many rate questions involve resolution of competing policies, and the ultimate objective is the establishment of a set of rates to accompany the firm into the future. Traditional litigation is as awkward in this context as it is in labor relations or any other ongoing contractual relationships where arbitration, for example, tends to have replaced formal lawsuits. Any analogy of public utility rate making to some other process soon breaks down; however, the point to stress is that rate making is substantially more sophisticated than most lawyers understand it to be.

Second, rate cases historically have been perceived to have a constitutional dimension. Traditionally, rate cases were litigated on the issue of the "taking" of the regulated firm's property. The law quite properly has insisted upon more formal

115

procedures where constitutional rights are at stake than where
they are not, and I believe this too has contributed to the
benefits (or baggage) of the present procedures. Without
in any sense belittling the importance of rate-making issues,
since the case of *Hope Natural Gas* we have moved to a substantially healthier view of rate-making cases as not presenting constitutional issues in the traditional sense of that
term. A regulated firm is certainly entitled as a matter of
law to reasonable rates, but the procedural methods we use to
determine these rates should not be the same as those used in
criminal justice.

Third, it is probably not irrelevant to point out that
utility rates have been falling over reasonably significant
periods during the last century. Even such a concept as
replacement-cost rate base valuation, now considered "liberal,"
was originally invented to justify the lowering of a firm's
rates in a time of deflation. Lawyers must take a great deal
of the blame for creating a system that served their regulated
clients well when it tended to delay the process by which such
rate decreases could be imposed. The procedures did not lead
to "optimal rate making" even then, of course, but it has taken
a shift to inflation as a long-term fact of life to bring home
the severity of the problem.

OPTIMAL DELAY IN RATE MAKING

What does it mean to have "procedural impediments to
optimal rate making?" The short answer is that it means that
the process comes out with the wrong answer because of the way
the process is structured. In practice, it usually means one
of three things: (1) the wrong questions are being asked,
(2) the wrong information is put before the decision makers,
or (3) there is such extensive delay in the system that even
when the answer is "right" it is so out of date that it is no
longer relevant.

To the extent that the first problem is true, economists
are to blame more than lawyers are. No matter how it may look
sometimes, lawyers are for the most part interested in
addressing the correct issues. Indeed it is partly through
programs such as the one that has culminated in this volume
and joint programs in law and economics at different univer-
sities that we attempt to reduce the problem of exploring the
wrong questions.

The second explanation falls more on lawyers' shoulders
since we tend to dictate what evidence can come before the
decision maker and what can not. Procedure also tends to dictate how carefully and at what point particular issues will be
raised and considered, and I believe that timing is critical
and basic to the question of improvement.

The third problem is the clearest area where lawyers must
address the need for change. We dictate, through procedures

that we develop, how long a case will take. If it takes too long by whatever appropriate standard one uses to make that determination, we have only ourselves to blame.

"Regulatory lag" is, of course, a common term. The phenomenon is the period of time between the experience of particular cost changes by a regulated firm and the time that its rates can reflect those new costs. However, that period is really composed of two parts--one substantive and one procedural. The substantive element is the conscious decision to make future rates turn on past costs. Inevitably, if next year's rates are based on last year's costs rather than on next year's costs, the rates will always be a year behind. Procedural delay, on the other hand, is that portion of the total period that is attributable to the sheer time it takes to process a rate case.

Both delays, of course, are to some extent created by lawyers. Substantive lag is in part a reflection of a lawyer's preference for hard evidence over opinions. To me, this aspect of "lag" is relatively easy to overcome by a change in the substantive principles to be applied in determining the proper test year. If change is to come, it will be when economists persuade lawyers that it should.

Procedural delay, on the other hand, is almost entirely our creation and overcoming it is up to the legal profession. The practical problems in accomplishing that are the primary focus of this chapter.

To complicate the matter further, I suggest that the consequences of regulatory delay are not necessarily all bad. The presence of a lag between experienced costs and allowed rates can create an incentive to keep the costs down. When costs were still declining, Bonbright advocated the use of delay as a device to give extra rewards to those firms that succeeded in lowering their costs below those on which the last rates were set. Comparable conclusions, for periods of rising costs as well, have been reached by others, the most prolific of which may be Elizabeth Bailey. Some recent writers, particularly Robert Spann, have made the point that a highly inflationary environment can turn a healthy incentive into a suffocating damper. All this simply points out that one need not approach the question of rate-making delay with the inevitable assumption that less is always better than more.

It would not be difficult to create a virtually delay-free regulatory system. Such a system might simply require that the company lay its tariff on a clerk's desk and have it rubber-stamped. There would be virtually no rate-making delay, but there would also be virtually no regulation. This simple illustration is used to make what I believe is a crucial point-- namely, that time is not the only relevant dimension of delay. At least equally important is the question of what one needs to know to achieve his regulatory objectives. The test of procedure, then, must be whether it helps get the maximum benefit from the regulatory effort expended. In the economics profession's jargon, the task must be to find that elusive moment when the marginal cost of more delay exceeds the marginal benefit from arriving at a more accurate determination of the relevant issues.

THE NATURE AND EXTENT OF CURRENT RATE-MAKING DELAY

Exact data on the nature and extent of delay in rate making are extremely difficult to obtain. I have recently been working on a study for the Administrative Conference of the United States to analyze delay in the four major federal rate-making agencies. I can only report that they do not know the extent of delay, and one suspects they do not really want to know. The same reaction has been found in state agencies and at the National Association of Railroad and Utility Commissioners (NARUC). Rate-making delay is something all agencies know exists but which most prefer not to specify too completely and thus not have to explain. However, some basic information can be developed to get a sense of the present situation.

1. The longest cases seem to be at the Federal Power Commission (FPC), where the 35 or so formal pipeline rate cases filed each year are now taking about four years to complete. The 100 wholesale electric rate cases each year at the FPC last about two years each.

2. Cases at the Federal Communications Commission (FCC) vary widely. The recent Dkt. 19129 on American Telephone and Telegraph (AT&T) rates took six years, and part of that time was under an acceleration order from the Court of Appeals. A case on private line tariffs has run five years with no end in sight. However, most cases now seem to be running about two years.

3. The Interstate Commerce Commission (ICC) has many more formal rate cases to decide, about 250 annually, but two years is the longest time usually required. Most cases take eight to nine months, while many others last about a year.

4. The few Civil Aeronautics Board (CAB) cases that go to full hearing take about two years each. Most, however, are handled informally and many of these take only a few months or less.

5. On the state level, the figures vary widely. A 1975 survey by NARUC reported that the average time for decision in major rate cases ranged from 2 months in Delaware to 2 years in West Virginia. Only eight other states admitted to taking a year or more, the majority taking from 8 to 11 months.

As suggested above, I think it is unrealistic to draw conclusions from this data alone. Everyone agrees that some reduction of time is desirable. The following, more revealing data (but even harder to develop) suggest where in the process the time is being consumed.

1. A look at major FPC electrical rate cases that were filed in 1974 and then went through full hearing and decision reveals that the cases took an average of 27 months, of which 12 were consumed in pre-hearing activity, 4 in hearing and briefing, 5 in preparing the initial decision, and 6 in the final decision.

2. Phase II of FCC Dkt. 19129 on American Telephone and Telegraph (AT&T) rates took 5 years. Of that, 28 months were consumed prior to hearing, 17 in hearings, 9 in issuing an initial decision, and 6 in a final decision.

3. An internal CAB study in 1972 found that cases were getting to hearing in about 4 months and took another 10 months to hear and get an initial decision. The board itself then sat on the cases another year before reaching a final decision.

4. Finally, a look at 18 months of Illinois Commerce Commission decisions (all under an 11-month statutory constraint) showed that it takes about 2.5 months to get a case to hearing. A hearing takes from 1 day to 7 months, the average being 3.7 months. There is no interim decision, but the commission's decision takes anywhere from 1 month to 7, the average being 3.8.

The point of all these numbers is that in most agencies the formal hearing is apparently not the place of greatest delay. The delay appears to come as the commission staff and interveners try to assimilate the relevant data prior to the hearing and as the decision makers try to come to terms with both data and policy issues at the close of the proceedings. In this light it may be possible to evaluate better some of the many "solutions" offered to the problem of delay.

SOME PROPOSED SOLUTIONS AND WHY THEY FALL SHORT

Solutions reducing the time required for deciding cases seem to be legion. One of the most common today is the establishment of arbitrary time limits within which the agency must reach a decision. Of the 51 jurisdictions noted in the 1975 NARUC survey, 38 (about 75 percent) had some such time limit whereas only 13 (25 percent) had none. The Railroad Revitalization and Regulatory Reform Act of 1976 has now introduced the concept into the federal system as well. The point of such rules is obvious, but the value of them is less so. If we were correct in assuming that time is not the only dimension of relevance in determining whether delay is excessive, then it may be true that some cases should take more than the maximum time while others should be decided in much less. Indeed, my informal reading of the Illinois experience suggests that time limits are indeed Procrustean. The biggest cases with the longest records are decided by the Commerce Commission in the last six weeks, while the short cases may take six months. This may be because the commissioners drop everything-- and properly so--to consider the big cases. It may also be that without time limits, tough cases would almost never get decided.

However, without trying to make a definitive determination of the value of time limits, it does seem that they treat only one part, the time dimension of the problem, and that more is required for a good solution.

A second practical effect of the fallacy of believing that time is the only relevant component of delay is the popularity of automatic adjustment clauses in whatever guise they may arise. In the previous chapter, Parker discusses his experience with the New Mexico plan, which seems to me to take the principle to its logical extreme. As a principle, however, automatic adjustment seems to me to constitute "nonregulation without deregulation." That is, all the limitations of entry and other protective devices of regulation are preserved without getting any of the benefits of a review of expenditures or valuations. Further, to the extent that such plans do not build-in incentives for efficiency, it will be difficult, even in retrospect, to tell how much harm was done. Automatic adjustments are, of course, attractive when companies are cash starved, and almost any concept would be seized upon if it would generate additional revenue. However, "optimal rate making"--that elusive goal-- can only be approached if we take seriously the objective of creating an incentive for economy and exercising a reasonable review of the wide range of basic issues underlying the firm's proposed rates. Time is an important dimension in which to measure delay, but again it is only a part of the story.

One of the favorite whipping boys for critics of rate-making dely are interveners in the rate proceeding. "If we only didn't have to deal with those self-appointed public interest groups," we sometimes hear, "we could avoid a lot of issues and save a lot of time." While that is an appealing thought, the negative influence of interveners is difficult to document. Here an important distinction should be drawn be- tween rate cases and licensing decisions, particularly nuclear plant sitings. In the latter, various "public interest" groups have been notorious (or heroic) in their ability to prolong a decision process far beyond what one would normally expect. In the rate-making area, however, their presence is much more to highlight issues that the commission should be, but often is not, considering. My observations of where delay occurs and my discussions with officials in rate-making agencies suggest to me that the marginal impact of interveners in the sense of prolonging the time of a case is very low. They rarely are the party allowed a continuance, for example. I am aware of Joskow's work suggesting that interveners make a significant difference in the results in rate cases. I do not dispute that and indeed would expect it to be true, but from my vantage point their participation in rate cases tends to be of the sort that leads to an improvement in the quality of results. Thus, the marginal cost in time and effort of their participation is probably justified.

The remaining proposals usually heard for rate-making reform tend to be much more technical in character. One line of reasoning calls for the increased judicializing of regulatory agency procedure. For example, some propose that all federal agencies (and presumably state agencies as well) should have uniform rules of procedure. Such proponents also often advocate that the discovery procedures before regulatory commissions be liberalized until they approach the liberality of the federal rules of civil procedure. My own view is that both of these proposals reflect a lawyer's bias that the more one makes something like a court, the better its decisions become. My experience and research suggest that few cases are seriously delayed because one or more of the parties do not understand the rules of procedure. Likewise, discovery, for all its virtues, is one of the greatest causes of or excuses for delay in our entire civil trial system. Further, excessive secrecy is rarely the problem in rate making in the same sense at least that it is in traditional litigation. The regulated firm seeking a rate increase is already required and usually eager to put forth as much information as one would normally need to know. Whether discovery should be permitted at times other than those in which a specific rate increase is requested is addressed below, but my view is that increasing the analogy of regulatory procedures to court procedures is a step in precisely the wrong direction.

The direct converse of these last proposals involves suggestions that decreased formality in procedure should be adopted. For example, some propose that only written evidence be received and thus that cross-examination be prohibited. The ICC quite successfully uses a form of this procedure that requires the parties to specify clearly in advance any controverted issues on which cross-examination will be useful. Such a procedure tends to minimize or eliminate the amount of time consumed in pointless cross-examination. The data cited above, however, suggest that comparatively little time in the total picture of rate-making delay is currently consumed by oral hearings. To the extent that data is available, and it is sparse, it appears that the largest amounts of time are consumed in writing opinions and considering the written evidence that has been submitted. Using all written evidence might help somewhat and in some cases, but it is too much to hope that it will greatly alleviate any delay problem.

Some simplifiers propose that agencies either use experts as decision makers or in lieu of the parties' witnesses. Thus, one official economist would make the "right" determination rather than having different economists spend so much time disagreeing, as is done in proceedings today. Although one can concede that there is undoubtedly some waste motion in any adversary proceeding, I am too much of a traditional lawyer to believe that the truth resides in only one "expert" and that consulting the oracle will inevitably lead to the best results. Agency experts may cut down the time required for litigation, but I am afraid they would tend to do so at the expense of mature consideration of the questions before the commission.

Among the most promising proposals are those to eliminate certain steps in the decision process. However, not everyone agrees what steps should be eliminated. Some, for example, would favor elimination of the decision by the hearing officer and submission of the case directly to the regulatory commission. Others, exactly to the contrary, would favor giving finality to the hearing officer's decision, subject only to appeal to the appointed body in cases of major importance. Still others propose creation of an intermediate review board between the hearing officer and the commission, whose job it would be to give an "automatic appeal" to any aggrieved party but presumably to do so quickly. Each of these proposals correctly perceives that it is the time for decision that appears to be the greatest element of delay today. It is also, however, one of the most difficult to correct.

One final matter that seems obvious but apparently is not is the need to track cases carefully and identify those where delay is occurring. Some state agencies with comparatively few cases may find such a system unnecessary, but until recently, the ICC, for example, relied on a few handwritten cards in a file drawer to keep track of its entire caseload. It was small wonder that cases could drag on for years and really not be noticed. The FCC and FPC still use a system that is similarly crude, and they simply rely on complaints from their victims to highlight problem areas. Both the ICC and CAB are moving to a system of computerized case management. Although there is no magic in such a system, it does allow virtually instant display of the status of any given case and the progress of any and all cases through the steps within the agency. Quite apart from any other proposals, such basic information is critical to reasonable case management.

A PROPOSED CHANGE IN THE STRATEGY OF RATE MAKING

Each of the proposals discussed above has been made con-scientiously by individuals of different opinions, and it may seem that I am casually dismissing our few best hopes for success. While the suggestions may have merit, I believe they share a common failing--a failing shared by the title of this chapter--namely, a belief that delay in rate-making procedure is caused primarily by a few procedural impediments. "Here is the cause," we say, as if removal of one or another barrier will make things right.

I submit that our task is different and that what is needed is a new strategy of rate making. The goal should be to bring maximum information to bear on relevant rate-making issues as quickly and clearly as possible. To do that requires three

fundamental, interrelated changes in the way rate making is
approached on both federal and state levels.

More Extensive Use of Rule Making

First, regulatory agencies should undertake a systematic
program of rule making with respect to issues of general
applicability. The standard model today is case-by-case
adjudication so typical of other legal decision making. In a
tort case, every plaintiff who seeks to recover, for example,
for the negligent design of a DC-10 airplane must prove that
negligent design in his or her lawsuit. Likewise, every
regulated firm wishing to use a particular form of accelerated
depreciation must prove the desirability of that form in each
case. It is true that in regulatory procedures, as in the
development of the common law, precedent is established from
one case to the next which makes it more or less likely that
a particular proposition will be easy to prove. However,
precedent is not uniformly binding, and the time required to
litigate, brief, and consider each issue in each case, not to
mention the uncertainty created for the regulated firms,
seems to me a major deterrent to optimal decisions.

Perhaps the best example of the alternative way of pro-
ceeding--the use of rule making as a predicate to the establishment of rates--is the Domestic Passenger Fare Investigation
(DPFI) at the CAB. This investigation was a multiyear project
in which the CAB attempted to think through most of the major
questions that recur in its decision process. Questions of
appropriate rate of return, the place of discount fares, the
appropriate fare taper, the relation of coach to first class,
and so on were all systematically addressed and conclusions
reached. Since the adoption of those rules, at least for general
rate increase requests, the CAB has been able to cut its case
processing time to almost nothing. Decisions are routinely
reached within the 30-day prenotice period, and thus the
effective date is not delayed. Some of the substantive elements
of the DPFI have been criticized by the Senate Subcommittee on
Administrative Practice and Procedure of the Senate Committee
on the Judiciary and others proposing airline deregulation, but
the procedural technique represented by CAB's effort is worthy
of emulation.

There is little question today that such procedures are
sanctioned by the courts. Whatever constitutional concerns
may once have existed about granting a firm the right to an
individualized hearing on its rate request have been satisfied
in the minds of the court by an opportunity of the regulated
firms to participate in the rule making decision process and to
raise any reasons why a rule should not apply in a given case.

Much of the law in this area has been made in cases where
the FCC has sought to rely on its earlier conclusions in the
Specialized Common Carrier case. In *Bell Telephone Co. of*

Pennsylvania v. *FCC*, for example, the Third Circuit Court of
Appeals summed up the considerations this way:

> First, . . . procedural flexibility can aid
> the FCC in making the substantive determina-
> tions that it is required to make under the
> Communications Act. . . . Second, . . . Congress
> has . . . [left] to the agency the determina-
> tion of the type of procedure to be employed
> in a given case. . . . Third, non-evidentiary
> rule making permits broad participation in
> the decision-making process and enables an
> administrative agency to develop integrated
> plans in important policy areas.

The last of these points seems to me particularly important. If we must have regulation, an agency cannot responsibly
avoid the task of frontally addressing fundamental issues.
However, it is next to impossible to do this in every case.
However, in a rule-making proceeding there is no way to avoid
it. Likewise, public interest groups or other interveners who
have felt it necessary to involve themselves routinely in rate
cases so as to protect a particular interest can, under a rule-
making procedure, focus their attention on the proceeding of
real concern to them. For example, one objector repeatedly
intervenes in CAB cases, alleging that the carrier and the
board are miscalculating the elasticity of demand for air
travel, and he always loses. He has asked that a rule-making
proceeding be instituted on the point. If he or his counter-
parts on other issues get their way in that proceeding, they
can be confident that the rule will be applied by the board
in later cases; if they do not get their way, they can seek
judicial review or legislative change. Indeed, an interesting
feature of this entire proposal is that it is often greeted
with the most acceptance by public interest groups that lawyers
often accuse of delay and that regulated firms charge with the
most resistance. Although speculating about motives is not
very fruitful, I do not think the point is without significance.
At least three major criticisms are sometimes raised
against this kind of proposal. First, agencies sometimes
argue that they would tie themselves down if they were required
to adhere to particular rules, even rules of their own making.
Flexibility is thought to be desirable by these agencies,
nominally because it allows them to adapt creatively to new
circumstances. To that complaint, one may respond that rule-
making is itself flexible--rules, once made, can be changed.
Further, "flexibility" is too often a euphemism for politically
oriented or inconsistent decision making. It creates an air
of ambiguity in which it is difficult for regulated firms to
act. To the extent that law serves a useful function in
utility regulation, I believe that predictability is one of

its most significant elements. The argument of loss of
flexibility, as the term is meant by most of its proponents,
seems to me to be an argument in favor of this proposal rather
than against it.

A second, more significant objection recognizes that it
is often difficult to sort out policy issues from the facts
out of which they arise. The FCC, for example, having stated
a general policy, must consider the problems of competition in
the telecommunications industry in the context of particular
tariff revisions. That is, each particular rate change request
has a broad policy impact, and it is extremely difficult to
decide the broad policy question in a vacuum. The FCC's response
has been to try to go both ways--i.e., to create a general
docket case to consider the broad issues while recognizing
that those issues will arise again in particularized form.
Actually, the FCC, with basically one regulatee, is probably
the least appropriate agency for getting into the general rule-
making approach, whereas AT&T has the understandable incentive
to test and retest the scope and limits of any rules. The
proposal should work much better in state agencies or federal
agencies having several smaller cases with recurring issues.
In such agencies, the potential for increased speed and full
consideration of the fundamental questions is enormous.

Third, it can be responsibly argued that the facts underlying the policy decisions change so frequently that general
principles are just not good for long. This kind of concern
has been raised about CAB's Domestic Passenger Fare Investigation, for example. It is argued that the rate of return conclusions are out of date, the load factor assumptions never
were very good, and that subsequent experience with discount
fares has undercut a great deal of what it took so long to
produce. This is a legitimate concern and probably true in
many circumstances. Each of these questions should be re-
examined on a systematic basis so as to review their current
soundness. Such a system would likely occupy significant
staff time and probably would not reduce the total effort within the agency in deciding rate-related issues. However, I
believe it would focus the commission's and the participant's
attention on specific substantive questions and thus both
improve decision quality and reduce the time required to process
any particular rate increase request.

Periodic Submission of Data

My first proposal toward a new rate-making strategy, then,
has been to approach the process, not solely as trial courts
approach tort cases, but with a healthy dose of rule making, at
least as to fundamental, recurring questions. The second major
change should involve significant improvement in the manner of
handling relevant cost data. Here, too, most regulatory
agencies still operate as do our trial courts. They take

evidence in an oral or typewritten form and let the decision maker see it only at or near the time when it must be taken under advisement. Yet the firms know the cost data well before this, and I believe that significant time savings as well as improvements in understanding could be achieved by providing these data in current form to the regulatory commission on a periodic basis as it is generated.

This appeal is not for a new record-keeping requirement on the part of the firms. Rather, since the information will have to be made available eventually, it might as well be sooner than later. The longer the commission and potential interveners have to look at the data in advance of the hearing, the less time need be wasted trying to assimilate and understand the data at a later time when it will contribute to delay.

This material can, and in most cases should, be made available in a computer-accessible form. In most situations it is already generated that way by the firm's own accounting process; ideally, a system would be developed in which a regulated firm would simply submit its basic cost information to the various bodies regulating it in a form that those commissions' computers can retrieve for any appropriate use during the year. I believe that a commission should be able to spot the need for a rate increase almost as early as the firm involved and ought to be in a position to rule on the matter without either undue delay or excessive reliance on the firm's representation or interpretation of the data.

Objections to this proposal seem relatively few. Some center around the practicality of generating the computer program, although this kind of work is already being done aggressively by the National Bureau of Standards in its Experimental Technology Incentives Program (ETIP), and a second approach is being developed at the FPC in its Automated Computer Regulatory Information System.

Other objections center on the practicality of developing uniform systems of accounts with sufficient sophistication to be able to deal with all forms of rate-making decisions. Cooperation in this direction has been significant between NARUC and federal agencies over the years, but even so there probably would be some cases in which individualized data would be required later. However, even a crude system would serve as a useful early warning device and would be better than the situation faced by most agencies today.

Encouragement of Settlement of Rate Cases

The third and final proposal for accelerating and improving agency decisions is probably the most controversial--the encouragement of case settlement. If delay at the decision-making stage is the critical problem today, it follows that simplifying or eliminating much of that decision process could significantly help reduce a commission's processing time.

Perhaps the best illustration of a settlement process is
that of the Federal Power Commission. Roughly 50 percent of
their contested rate cases are now ultimately settled in this
way; in addition, they are settled before formal hearings and
are resolved in approximately two years, in contrast to those
that go to full hearing and take about four years. The FPC
is making a strenuous effort to increase the number of settlements today, and the ultimate success of that program will
be important for all of us.

Most of the resistance to settlement seems to arise from
the concern that a case that is settled is almost by definition
"wrongly decided." That is, if the case is settled on terms
other than those that would have been reached in a final
decision, the decision to that extent is wrong. The fallacy,
of course, is assuming that the decision after a full proceeding would have been "right." The fact is that the rate-
making process is ultimately judgmental in any event, and
there is in most cases a range of possible decisions that are
reasonable. A settlement within that range is about as likely
to be "right" as a final decision, and, to the extent that the
result is reached more promptly and at less cost, virtually
everyone comes out ahead.

The role of the commission under this approach would not
be, as tends to be true today, primarily to make final decisions. Rather, it is to structure and to preside over a rate-
making process that is fundamentally adversary in nature. In
this sense, the agency would be borrowing something constructive
from the modern trial court. Today, the vast majority of
cases on the docket of a trial judge is settled by the parties.
Settlements are arrived at on the basis of some assessment of
the result that would be reached if one side were intransigent
and the case went to trial. However, most cases do not reach
that stage, not only because the courts are crowded, but because all sides recognize the expense of litigation and the
reality that justice delayed is justice denied.

At least two different kinds of situations need to be
distinguished in regard to settlement. First is the situation
in which the parties to the case are both private firms with
adverse interests and the agency's role is really analogous
to that of a court. A good example of this is the FPC's
wholesale electric rate cases, and it is perhaps not surprising
that settlement of such cases has been relatively easy. The
other situation represents the larger number of cases; in
these, the regulated firm is the proponent of change and the
regulatory agency is the adversary party. This is the more
familiar regulatory posture, but even here, interveners and
customers with adverse interests are often sufficient foils
to make the situation quite analogous to the first.

The more serious problem lies in guaranteeing that all
parties who would be affected by the final decision are represented in the settlement. In large multiparty cases this can

be particularly difficult, and minor differences could destroy an entire settlement effort. The courts have properly concluded, however, that if a party reasonably representative of each contesting interest approves the settlement, then there is a basis for assuming that it is proper.

The lingering problem, of course, is that not every interest is always represented by a party and that one or more decisions reached by settlement might be "unfair" in significant ways. To deal with this problem, I would have the commission assume the responsibility that a trial judge assumes today in class action suits and negotiated guilty plea cases. That is, the burden of initiating the settlement and defining its terms should fall on the affected parties, but the decision maker should have a residual and significant burden of guaranteeing that the result is fair. The analogy between class action cases, guilty pleas, and the process of proper rate regulation seems to be really quite close. In each case, there can be an assumption that the details of the arrangement can best be understood and worked out by the parties themselves, but there is a public interest (or an interest of unrepresented members of the class) that it is the responsibility of the court to see does not go unrecognized. The prime objection today at the FPC seems to be the delay in approving final settlements. Such delay is probably inevitable if the review process is to be taken seriously, but it should be minimized if settlements are to be further encouraged.

CONCLUSION

All three parts of this "new strategy" in rate making need to be implemented if any are to be really effective. That is, settlement can be justified if, and probably only if, it is consistent with rules arrived at in rule-making proceedings, participation in which was open to all and which were subject to judicial review, and if the result is consistent with the data on file with the regulatory commission and available to all parties and the reviewing court. Likewise, rule making may not be a truly cost-effective exercise if the parties cannot take the rules, use them to predict with confidence the ultimate result of a hearing, and then short-circuit the need for a hearing by settling in advance.

It would be presumptuous of me to suggest that these three steps would lead to "optimal rate making". That can only be a goal. Although panaceas are easier to describe than implement, almost everyone agrees that something must be done. I am hopeful that this proposal or one like it can help achieve that elusive goal of effective regulation, participation by all affected groups, and maximum possible speed in the decision of rate-making cases.

7
New Economics in Energy

Eric J. Schneidewind

A relatively young regulator discussing the "new economics in energy" is bound to be aware of an age-old paradox first described by Plato. This paradox centers around the fact that "men of thought," exemplified by academicians and professional economists, often abandon the field of government and hence the field of regulation to young and relatively inexperienced people such as myself who may be loosely described as "men of action."

If, as Plato tells us, this paradox has existed since the age of Pericles, I do not propose to set matters straight in the course of one chapter in a volume. I do, however, wish to expose economists in the field of regulation to a new trend that may affect their lives and will certainly affect the area of regulatory economics. I will use certain specific programs as examples of this new trend in regulation, but these programs in and of themselves are not important. The important point I wish to make is that new economic conditions have set the stage for a radical change in the way energy utilities do business. If economists are not careful, men of action will dominate this process of change without the counsel and wisdom that can be provided by men with training in the economics of regulation.

Even amateur economists like myself know that rapid price changes in any vital commodity usually cause a series of actions and reactions throughout the economy. Since 1973, the cost of energy has increased dramatically. I will not detail the reasons for this increase, but I think that readers of this chapter will be particularly aware that the problem of increasing energy costs cannot be blamed exclusively on OPEC or any other single factor.

Ideally, a regulator's task is to react as quickly and effectively as possible to these rapidly changing price signals. As a first step in developing a course of action to mitigate the impact of these price increases, a regulator must look at the relationship between energy price and use. If we assume that our society has reacted effectively to the old, low energy price, we have to assume that, all things being equal, the devices and processes that use energy have effectively balanced the cost of energy with the cost of reducing energy consumption.

If this assumption is correct, major energy price increases justify significant new expenditures in the area of energy conservation. As an example, if the average home heating bill is $200, installation of about $275 worth of ceiling insulation can reduce gas consumption as much as 17 percent, or about $34 per year. At this rate, the energy savings produced by ceiling insulation would barely cover the yearly interest charges on a 12 percent, four-year $275 loan. However, as soon as home heating bills increase to about $500, the savings produced by ceiling insulation increase to about $85 per year. At this rate, savings produced by ceiling insulation can more than repay the cost of a 12 percent, four-year loan to install the insulation.

This basic example illustrates a well-known but often ignored principle: conservation does not make sense unless there is a proper relationship between the price of the item being conserved and the price of the conservation measures. Like so many other adages, however, application of this principle does not produce accurate results unless accurate assumptions are used. In this specific case, one must ask what is meant by the "price of the item being conserved"? In other words, when a homeowner installs ceiling insulation, exactly what costs are being avoided by the homeowner, and, more important, what costs are being subtracted or added to costs borne by the entire body of gas customers. In the case of ceiling insulation, we know that the homeowner is avoiding an annual cost equal to the cost of about 34 Mcf of gas a year. At today's prices, that is about $75 or $80.

SYSTEM COSTS

The homeowner's reduced consumption can also result in increased costs to all gas customers. This phenomenon occurs when conservation reduces the total volume of gas over which certain fixed costs may be spread. An example of this phenomenon occurred recently in California when voluntary reductions in water use resulted in increased unit costs due to the necessity of spreading the fixed costs of the plant over a greatly reduced volume of water sold.

This effect, however, need not occur in the case of an energy form such as natural gas which is in high demand. The gas conserved by a homeowner may be used by an existing customer or a new customer, in which case no extra costs would be spread over the system. If a new customer were added to the system who used gas conserved by the first homeowner, the extra costs associated with serving a new customer would be added to total system costs and would be offset by a service charge to the new customer.

130

POTENTIAL SYSTEM BENEFITS

Although conservation can result in increased unit costs
of energy in a relatively "closed" energy distribution system,
in reality, energy distribution systems do not function as
closed systems. It is this fact that may cause individual
conservation to result in significant benefits to all customers
of an energy distribution system.

The phenomenon of rising costs of incremental supplies of
energy has become a fact of life for most energy utilities.
This situation has caused many economists to propose pricing
structures that charge new customers the full and generally
higher costs of obtaining new supplies of energy to serve them.
Of course, many economists argue that the cost of more expensive new sources of energy should be "rolled in" to the costs
of all energy sold to all customers.

In a sense, conservation can result in the exact opposite
of incremental pricing. Conservation can allow an energy
distribution utility to avoid purchasing additional, more
expensive supplies of energy if the utility declines to contract for expensive new sources of energy or is able to opt
out of existing contracts and the utility wishes to continue
serving existing customers or wishes to add new customers.
As shown below, utility investments in conservation may
"produce" more gas per dollar than equivalent investments in
new gas exploration.

If a utility wishes to curtail existing customers,
"conservation gas" may have to be sold. Depending upon the
price received for this gas, conservation may or may not result
in lower unit costs to all customers. If individual conservation can result in lower costs for all energy customers, it
may be logical for an energy utility to subsidize or otherwise
encourage individual conservation among its customers.

GAS UTILITIES--A TALE OF TWO THEORIES

There are two dominant theories regarding the proper
method of evaluating the worth to a gas company of a gas
conservation program. One theory, advanced by existing large
users of natural gas, contends that the cost of a conservation
program should include the adverse impact on the cost per unit
of gas caused by spreading fixed distribution system costs over
the smaller volume of sales that occurs as a result of conservation. These theorists argue that use of conservation gas
to serve new customers is counterproductive because these new
customers would be served equally well with purchases of new
gas and that this additional volume of new gas entering the
system would actually lower the cost of gas for all customers
by spreading fixed costs over a larger volume of sales.

There are cynics who say that existing gas customers who
hold this theory know that (1) there are no long-term additional

131

supplies of gas available and (2) that unsubsidized conservation efforts will make large additional supplies of natural
gas available if gas utilities can be persuaded to refuse
service to new customers and curtail service to existing
customers that use gas for low priority purposes.

A second theory contends that gas conservation programs
should be judged primarily by the volume of gas "produced" per
dollar of capital investment and by the cost of known, alternative, long-term supplies of natural gas (such as Artic gas
or Algerian gas). These theorists argue that demand for gas
always exceeds supply and that there is always a market for
all the short-term and long-term supplies of gas that a utility
can obtain. In view of this situation, a gas utility will
seldom pass up conventional sources of gas in order to implement a conservation program. Thus, a utility will always flow
the maximum amount of gas possible through its system, thereby
producing a maximum reduction of fixed costs per unit of gas
sold. Conservation programs are therefore to be evaluated as a
means of extending service to new customers or of continuing
service to old customers at a price that should closely approxi-
mate the investment that a utility must make in order to provide service with conventional sources of gas.

ELECTRIC UTILITIES

In the case of electric utilities, an investment in customers' conservation measures should equal or exceed the
variable costs (fuel) and fixed cost (new plant construction)
that can be avoided minus the increased costs per unit of
electricity caused by a reduced sales volume over which existing fixed cost can be spread. Varying electric load patterns
by time of day and by season complicate this judgment as do the
varying types of fuel that are burned by different generating
plants. In addition, load control options such as interruptible
service must be considered as effective conservation measures
because these options usually enable a utility to avoid operation
of fuel-inefficient peaking generation units.

Most of the principles discussed thus far are fairly well
known to economists who have been interested in the gas and
electric utility industries during the past few years. Only
recently, however, have concrete proposals begun to be formu-
lated that would combine these principles into practical programs that could be implemented by energy utilities. In the
remainder of this chapter, I will describe and critique several
of these proposed programs.

SELECTED GAS INDUSTRY PROGRAMS

Michigan Consolidated Gas Company

In 1975, the Michigan Consolidated Gas Company suggested

132

that a surcharge be placed on each unit of gas sold and that
the proceeds be paid directly to residential customers as a
bonus for implementing conservation measures. This proposal
was criticized as being administratively unworkable and containing little concrete justification for the specific level
of incentive payments contained in the proposal.

In the absence of specific data on the type and cost of
alternative gas sources that need not be purchased because of
conservation, it is difficult to evaluate the merits of this
program. The program might be justified on the basis that
without conservation, alternative gas supplies might not be
available and some existing customers might have to be curtailed
or cut off.

Orange and Rockland Utilities, Inc.

On June 11, 1976, Orange and Rockland Utilities, Inc., of
New York requested permission to institute a pilot Energy Conservation and Reallocation Program. Orange and Rockland had
been unable to attach new customers for the previous year due
to the inability of its suppliers to provide adequate amounts
of gas. In order to serve new customers, Orange and Rockland
worked out an arrangement whereby six new customers could
obtain gas service by insulating or encouraging the insulation
of existing Orange and Rockland gas-heating residential customers. These six new customers could receive gas service as
soon as they could demonstrate that the installation of conservation measures that they had installed in the homes and
businesses of Orange Rockland customers would save as much
gas as the six new customers would use.

The Orange and Rockland pilot program is a good example
of a conservation program that benefits all customers of the
utility. Since the six new customers would purchase the
conserved gas at existing prices, existing customers would
not pay for the increased per unit fixed costs that can result
from a reduction of sales caused by conservation. In addition,
since alternate sources of gas were not available, the existing
Orange and Rockland customers would not lose the opportunity
to lower their gas bills in an amount equal to the reduction in
fixed costs per unit of gas caused by the flow of additional
volumes of gas through the existing distribution system.

In theory, the Orange and Rockland program offered substantial benefits to some customers and no drawbacks to existing customers. In practice, the program proved unworkable.
The six customers who were offered participation in the program
were not able or were unwilling to stimulate the required level
of conservation. Two additional sets of six customers were
given the same option, and they also failed to encourage the
necessary conservation measures that would have allowed them
to obtain service.

133

James Tanner's Home Insulation Incentive Program

In the October 21, 1976, edition of *Public Utilities Fortnightly*, James Tanner, supervising engineer for Pacific Gas and Electric Company, proposed an extremely innovative gas conservation program. Tanner proposed that in gas systems with declining or stable gas supplies, gas customers who are being curtailed or who require additional gas supplies could literally bid for the gas saved by residential customers. Mr. Tanner noted that initial capital investment is currently the greatest barrier to residential gas conservation. Typically, an investment in conservation measures such as ceiling insulation does not "pay off" for six or seven years.

Tanner reasoned that for certain commercial and industrial customers, the gas saved by residential conservation often has a "true" or unregulated value far in excess of its regulated prices. Typically, such customers must use electricity, propane, or No. 2 oil as alternate fuels when gas is not available. If these customers would pay for "conservation gas" at a price in excess of the regulated market price of gas, the difference between regulated and unregulated gas prices could be paid to residential customers as an added inducement to invest in conservation measures.

Tanner suggested that such a system could work if commercial and industrial customers bid for supplies of conservation gas through a gas utility. A gas utility could collect the bid monies and pay an amount equal to the difference between bid price and regulated price to gas customers who had contracted with the utility and agreed to install conservation measures. In effect, certain commercial or industrial customers would be buying part of the right of residential customers to use virtually unlimited amounts of natural gas.

Although Tanner's proposal is a bit complex, it would prove equitable and beneficial to all gas customers because the direct costs of the program are borne by the direct beneficiaries of the program. To evaluate the cost of this program properly, a specific gas company would have to be used as an example. If this company had access to large, long-term new supplies of gas, existing customers might be losing a chance to have fixed costs spread over a larger volume of sales and thus reduce all gas bills. If, on the other hand, no long-term supplies were available or if such new gas supplies cost more than the retail price of gas plus the "excess" price necessary to encourage residential conservation, all of a gas utility's customers would be better off under the Tanner plan. To my knowledge, no utility has implemented the Tanner plan.

Niagara-Mohawk Plan

The Niagara-Mohawk Gas Company of New York currently uses

134

a novel and reportedly successful program to augment their gas supply during periods of shortage. This program exploits the fact that many of Niagara-Mohawk's current industrial customers have voluntarily developed the capacity to burn oil as well as gas. (During the past few years, Niagara-Mohawk has required large new customers to have this capability as a condition of service. Presumably, these newer customers may be interrupted during periods of gas shortage.)

In order to mitigate the impact of short-term gas shortages, Niagara-Mohawk interrupts service to its older industrial customers with dual fuel capability. These older customers burn their supplies of oil, which is more expensive than gas, and Niagara-Mohawk delivers the gas thus made available to industrial gas customers that do not have the capability to burn alternate fuels. In return for using the gas "given up" by their older industrial customers, Niagara-Mohawk makes cash payments to these customers in an amount equal to the difference between the customer's actual cost for an alternate fuel (oil) and the estimated cost of gas to meet the same requirement. This system allows Niagara-Mohawk literally to increase its available gas supply by almost 3 percent or 3 billion cubic feet during periods of gas shortage. This program could cost Niagara-Mohawk's customers as much as $3 million per year (assuming that the maximum difference in cost between oil and gas is about $1/Mcf), but this would still be preferable to shutting off customers that had no dual fuel capability.

This program would be more expensive to Niagara-Mohawk's customers than purchasing new short-term supplies of gas if the gas costs less than about $3/Mcf, because these new supplies of gas could be used to spread system fixed costs over a greater volume of sales. Generally speaking, however, large volumes of short-term or long-term gas have not been available to New York utilities, so the Niagara-Mohawk solution appears to have many of the benefits of programs that reduce volume permanently by conservation or cut off and programs that produce a low cost of gas by spreading fixed costs over large sales volumes.

The Michigan Public Service Commission (MPSC) Conservation Plan

In a program released in December 1976, the MPSC proposed that gas utilities literally give away insulation and other conservation devices to their residential customers.[1] The rationale for this plan was that a yearly investment of $117 million by Michigan's gas utilities on a statewide basis could insulate all gas-using homes in Michigan as well as retrofit all of Michigan's residential gas furnaces and result in the conservation of 80 million Mcf of gas per year for a cost of about $1.46 for every thousand cubic feet of gas saved by this program. Naturally, the gas saved by this plan could be sold to other customers. Even before President Carter's proposal to increase newly discovered gas prices to $1.75/Mcf, a utility wishing to buy and distribute new sources of natural gas from wells drilled in the continental United States had to pay $1.44/Mcf. Even more dramatic, gas from Alaska or Algeria is projected to cost between $3.50 and $4.00/Mcf. In other words, by giving away residential conservation devices, a utility could obtain gas to sell at a lower cost than by drilling a well or bringing in the gas from Alaska or Algeria.

The Revised Michigan Public Service Commission (MPSC) Interest-Free Loan Program

The initial proposal was the subject of public hearing in early March 1977. As a result of information developed in these public hearings, the staff of the Michigan Public Service Commission released a revised gas utility conservation program on May 9, 1977. The revised program called for gas utilities to provide ten-year, no down payment, no interest loans to their customers that would be used to purchase certain gas conservation devices and ceiling insulation. The proposal contended that the approximately $44 million annual interest subsidies that such a program would cost on a statewide basis could increase Michigan's total gas supply 9.5 percent at a cost per unit of gas (52¢) that was less than gas produced from wells. This program would also lower residential gas bills from 15 to 21 percent (depending upon the price of gas) even after the resident repaid the yearly cost of his interest-free conservation loan. According to the revised program, costs would be spread over all utility customers on the theory that the increased gas supply would prevent curtailment and would cost less than purchasing alternate gas supplies.

The MPSC May 9, 1977, proposal is based upon the assumption that a gas utility could sell large new supplies of gas at a price equal to or greater than current price levels or that, alternatively, the cost of the new supply of "conservation gas" will be lower than the cost of obtaining gas from other feasible sources. Under virtually any economic test, the gas produced by the MPSC program will be available at a lower cost than Arctic, Algerian, or synthetic gas. (Michigan utilities or pipelines are in the process of contracting for or using Arctic and synthetic gas.)

The utility investment necessary to "produce" gas under the MPSC program is about 52¢/Mcf as contrasted to a projected interstate price for "new" gas of about $1.75. On the other hand, any new gas supply would lower the fixed costs per unit of gas by spreading these costs over a larger volume of sales. Since large new supplies of gas from the continental United States are not available to Michigan utilities, rolling in supplies of gas at $1.75/Mcf is simply not an option.

In the absence of large, long-term supplies of new gas produced from conventional sources in the continental United States, the MPSC program is a far less expensive means of supplying gas than any other alternative.

Michigan Consolidated Gas Company

In June 1977, Michigan Consolidated Gas Company filed a formal request that the Michigan Public Service Commission approve their participation in an interest-free, no down payment conservation loan program that conforms with the general principles of the MPSC's revised program of May 9, 1977.

Consumers Power Company

In July 1977, Consumers Power Company announced that they had requested formal MPSC approval of a new gas conservation program. Consumers Power Company's proposed program is unusual in several respects. The program is intended to "produce" enough gas to enable Consumers to resume connection of new residential and commercial gas customers. Basically, all gas saved through their program will be dedicated to serving these new customers.

The Consumers program will make long-term conservation loans available to their customers at interest rates that will be so low that the customer's gas savings will exceed the annual cost of the loan. Thus, gas customers with very low incomes would be able to participate in this program. The interest costs on these loans will be subsidized by a surcharge placed on the cost of gas sold to the new residential and commercial customers who were connected as a result of the conservation program. Thus, the persons benefiting directly from this conservation program would be paying for all costs of the program.

Since all conserved gas will be sold to new customers, gas prices to existing customers will not increase to compensate for fixed charges being spread over reduced volumes of gas. Also, since no new, long-term gas supplies are available to Consumers, existing customers did not have the opportunity to experience the rate reduction that occurs when increased demand is met by new, additional supplies of gas that in turn allow fixed costs to be spread over larger sales volumes.

Lake Superior District Power Company

In Michigan, the Lake Superior District Power Company recently suggested that the gas turbines currently being used to pump gas through pipelines be replaced by electrically driven pumps. Lake Superior stated that electrically driven pumps generally cost no more to use than natural gas-driven turbine pumps. Since gas-driven pipeline pumps use approximately 10 percent of total pipeline throughput, available gas supplies could be increased 10 percent by converting to electric or oil-driven pumps.

Lake Superior has converted one of their pumps to a dual oil-gas capability to allow additional peak-day deliveries by switching to oil as a pump fuel. Lake Superior claims that electrically driven pumps on the gas pipeline would cost no more than natural gas-powered pumping if the gas used for this purpose were priced at market costs rather than the artifically low price authorized by the Federal Power Commission. If their contention is correct, most pipelines and gas distribution companies could increase their available gas supplies by as much as 10 percent at no long-term increased cost to the company and at a reduced cost to their customers owing to the impact of 10 percent more gas volume available to offset fixed costs.

These programs have created a significant new role for Michigan's gas companies and for gas companies all over the United States. Statewide application of the MPSC program could involve as much as $1 billion of investment. Regulators who are interested in providing the lowest cost, reliable source of energy to gas-consuming citizens must face the challenge of enabling and encouraging gas utilities to shift their role from production by conventional means to production by cost-effective but unconventional means such as conservation.

This task will not be easy. Gas utilities are organized to find gas under the ground and bring it to market, not to insulate ceilings. Neither are gas customers accustomed to a utility that concerns itself with home insulation as well as exploration and drilling.

ELECTRIC INDUSTRY PROGRAMS

Some electric utilities have already begun to use or research unconventional means of providing their customers with electric service. Use of interruptible residential air conditioning offers an example of a situation where an unconventional approach offers significant opportunities to reduce electrical energy costs.

Detroit Edison Interruptible Air Conditioning Experiments

Currently, Detroit Edison is testing radio control equipment that can turn off residential air conditioners during periods of peak demand. A system that turned off all of Edison's residential central-air conditioners for 15 minutes each hour could reduce Edison's system peak by about 200 MW. At current prices, that additional 200 MW of capacity could cost as much as $180 million to build. A system that permitted Edison to turn off all residential central air conditioners during the entire period of a peak or an emergency would reduce Edison's needed capacity by 400 MW. This capacity could otherwise cost as much as $360 million to build. Preliminary studies show that the equipment used to achieve ripple

138

control of air conditioners could be installed for a fraction of the cost of the generating capacity it could eliminate.

Tennessee Valley Authority Interest-Free Loans

Recently, the Tennessee Valley Authority (TVA) announced a program to provide their customers with interest-free home insulation loans and free energy audits. The interest-free loans are being offered to encourage electric-heating customers to insulate their ceilings to R-19 levels.

The TVA is paying the interest on these loans on the theory that the reduced use of electricity will enable the TVA to reduce purchases of power and operation of peaking units and to reduce the amount of new generating capacity needed to serve their customers. In other words, the TVA has found that subsidies of residential conservation are a more cost-efficient means of "producing" electricity than purchasing or generating electricity.

CONCLUSION

In the long run, energy regulation must be pragmatic instead of traditional. We must channel resources into areas that deliver the most cost-effective sources of energy. There will be initial resistance to this new role for utility companies despite the fact that customers expect their utilities to develop energy sources at the lowest possible cost. As energy costs increase, it is safe to predict that the role of utilities and regulators will become even more unconventional in an attempt to react to these price increases.

I am quite sure that many readers are saying to themselves, "This is just another conservationist who is more interested in no-growth economics than energy production." Rather, as I contended at the outset of this chapter, I consider myself to be a pragmatist who is merely looking for reliable, inexpensive sources of energy.

The key question facing many regulators today is whether the institutional and legal barriers surrounding public utilities will allow those utilities to pursue the unconventional but cost-effective energy "production" methods that will become increasingly attractive as energy prices rise.

I believe that these questions will pose a severe challenge to regulation in the coming years. Perhaps this challenge will be overshadowed by other and more severe problems, but perhaps the benefits and institutional strains created by these unconventional means of energy production will change the role of utilities as we now know them.

NOTE

1. This proposal has been called the "Rosenberg

proposal," although the MPSC announced the program several
weeks before Mr. Rosenberg announced his proposal and the
MPSC commenced work on this program several months before
Mr. Rosenberg commenced work on his program. During research
for this chapter, however, I discovered a July 1, 1976, article
by Edward F. Ranshaw of the Department of Economics of the State
University of New York at Albany in which the author suggested
that utilities give away conservation materials and place
the cost of these materials in their rate base.

Index

Denver Research Institute, 60
Deregulation, 64, 70-74, 75, 83, 123
Detroit Corporation Counsel, 42
Detroit Edison, 138
Domestic Passenger Fare Investigation (DPFI), 123, 125
Dupree, Walter G., Jr., 60

Eberle, David W., 114
Edison Electric Institute-Electric Power Research Institute
    study, 17
Eisenhower, Dwight D., 42
Electricity pricing, 1-39, 97-114
Emergency Natural Gas Act, 50, 68, 69, 78
Energy crisis, 6
Energy, Department of, 87
Energy Research and Development Administration, 59, 61
England, 17, 19
Environmental Defense Fund (EDF), 4, 5, 83, 84, 88
Erickson, Edward W., 44
Experimental Technology Incentives Program (ETIP), 126

Faulhaber, G. R., 23, 39
Federal Communications Commission (FCC), 118, 122, 123, 124, 125
Federal Energy Administration (FEA), 6, 12, 14, 15, 17, 30, 34,
    35, 59, 60, 61, 65, 66, 67, 69, 76
Federal Energy Regulatory Commission, 89
Federal Power Commission (FPC), 41, 42, 43, 46, 47, 48, 49,
    50, 55, 57, 58, 59, 60, 61, 67, 68, 69, 70, 73, 74, 79, 80,
    85, 86, 118, 119, 122, 126, 127, 128, 138
Feldstein, Martin, 23, 39
Ford Foundation, 59, 60
France, 13, 17, 19
Future Requirements Committee, 59, 60

Gas. *See* Natural gas
Geist, Gerry D., 113
General Accounting Office (GAO), 73, 74, 78, 81
Gillen, William J., 29, 38
Goldman, M. B., 23, 24, 38, 39
Green, William H., 20, 21
Green Tariff, 13
Gross National Product (GNP), 70

Habicht, Ernst, 88
Harris-Fulbright Act, 42
Harvard Institute of Economic Research, 60
Hawkins, Clark A., 80
Helms, Robert B., 80
Homan, Paul T., 60
Hope Natural Gas Co. (Federal Power Commission v.), 116
Hudson, Edward A., 60

Ranshaw, Edward F., 140
Rate-making delay, 117-122, 128
Regulatory lag, 97, 101, 110, 111, 112, 117
Regulatory reviews, 2, 3
Resources for the Future, 59, 60
Robison, Albert J., 113
Rochester Gas and Electric Co., 86
Rolled-in pricing, 71, 87, 88, 89, 131
Roseman, Herman G., 113
Rosenberg, William G., 139, 140
Russell, Milton, 67, 68, 81

Schneidewind, Eric J., 129
Schurr, Sam H., 60
Senate Subcommittee on Administrative Practice and
  Procedure, 123
Shepherd, William G., 19, 22
Sibley, David S., 23, 24, 38, 39
Sierra Club, 4
Smoensky, Paul, 29, 38
SNG (synthetic natural gas), 85, 136
Spann, Robert, 44, 117
Specialized Common Carrier case, 123
Spence, A. M., 23, 39
Standard and Poor's Utility Stock Index, 104, 105
Stanford Research Institute, 59
Starratt, Patricia E., 44
Steele, Henry B., 60
Stelzer, Irwin, 110, 113

Tanner, James, 134
Tarif Vert, 19
Tax credits, 69
Taylor, Lester D., 20, 22, 25, 30, 39, 65, 66, 81
Tennessee Valley Authority (TVA), 139
Texas, 50, 55, 56
Time-of-day rates. *See* Peak load pricing

United States Geological Survey (USGS), 55, 57

Verleger, P., 25, 39
Vermont, 12

Waberman, Leonard, 44
Washington Gas Light Co., 90
Weisser, Mendel, 23, 39
Wenders, John T., 20, 22
West, James A., 60
West Virginia, 118
Wisconsin, 13
Wisconsin Power and Light Company, 12
Wisconsin Public Service Commission, 18, 19, 42, 84